MAX REGER'S MUSIC FOR SOLO PIANO

D1616619

MAX REGER'S MUSIC FOR SOLO PIANO

AN INTRODUCTION

Helmut Brauss

THE UNIVERSITY OF ALBERTA PRESS

First published by
The University of Alberta Press
Athabasca Hall
Edmonton, Alberta
Canada T6G 2E8

Copyright © The University of Alberta Press 1994

ISBN 0–88864–255–5 paper

CANADIAN CATALOGUING IN PUBLICATION DATA

Brauss, Helmut, 1930–
Max Reger's music for solo piano

Includes bibliographical references and index.
ISBN 0–88864–255–5

1. Reger, Max, 1873–1916—Criticism and interpretation.
I. Title.
ML410.R25B72 1994   780'.92   C94–910673–9

Title page photograph:
Reger, München, 1907. Foto
Veritas, München. (Max
Reger Institut)

Printed on acid-free paper. ∞

Printed and bound in
Canada by Quality Color
Press, Inc., Edmonton,
Alberta, Canada

All rights reserved.

No part of this publication may be produced, stored in a retrieval system, or transmitted in any forms or by any means, electronic, mechanical, photocopying,
recording, or otherwise, without the prior permission of the copyright owner.

The University of Alberta Press would like to acknowledge, with gratitude, the
financial support provided by the Alberta Foundation for the Arts, a beneficiary of
the Lottery Fund of the Government of Alberta.

COMMITTED TO THE DEVELOPMENT OF CULTURE AND THE ARTS

CONTENTS

AUGUSTANA UNIVERSITY COLLEGE
LIBRARY

PIECES SELECTED FOR DISCUSSION

Pieces Selected for Discussion

FOREWORD

The work of Max Reger has always been judged in a curiously general way. The feverish controversy among his contemporaries, who either condemned his destructive influence on music or praised him as a guarantor of the future, gave way after his death to a paralysing indifference that has extended into our recent time, particularly within countries beyond the German-speaking area. Reger perpetually has been judged rather than explored. A widespread ignorance of his work has been hidden behind preconceived opinions. From Reger's time to the present, the status of his complex oeuvre has been determined by its susceptibility to a one-sided selective analysis.

With his discussion of the works for solo piano, however, Helmut Brauss is trying to change this situation. After years of practical familiarity with the oeuvre and its interpretation, he sees his pedagogical task as a university professor aware of the problem of disseminating material that is not secured by an interpretive tradition, and that is unknown to most students, to be to facilitate the selection from a multitude of uneven material and to encourage students to take a guided approach to this matter.

Max Reger created a legion of works of widely diverging quality under unimaginable self-inflicted pressures. Masterworks like the *Bach Variations*, by themselves guaranteeing Reger's immortality, are found beside occasional compositions that were sometimes not even acceptable to the composer himself. More than the excessive haste of the creative process, which by itself did not prevent masterworks, it was in many cases the lack of inner motivation that caused embarrassing solutions. Works often were written in compliance with his publishers' demands for products that would sell and at the same time complement main works considered unplayable. However, even under such restricted circumstances some important creations—sometimes suitable for pedagogical purposes—came into being, to which the author draws the reader's attention.

Reger's work is not comprehensible outside its historical context. Since he received essential inspiration from other composers, from J.S. Bach to his own contemporaries, analysis was often conveniently biased towards comparisons with known predecessors. Contrary to such a procedure, the author of this volume approaches the work directly and without any detours, to see the originality and the specific language into which all influences flowed. Brauss guides one's view to the "vocabulary" of Reger's diction, which must be studied like a foreign language in order to be understood. That particular vocabulary includes the revolutionary chromatic harmony and traditional, highly conscious contrapuntal procedures derived from Bach, as well as a nonperiodic shaping of melody, and the firm frame of traditional forms.

The author sees the relevance of the interpretation as such as an equally important part of the compositional process among other "substantial" means of composition. This is the most important message to the player and pedagogical guidance given to the student.

The immense complexity of all parameters of Reger's compositional procedures must be complemented by an intelligently flexible interpretation that should encompass tempo changes, dynamic tension and relaxation curves, and sophisticated and meaningful articulations, as well as the extreme fluctuations of expression and mood. If this introduction to Max Reger's music for solo piano succeeds in generating an understanding of the necessity of that type of flexibility, one need not worry about the future of Reger's piano music.

Dr. Susanne Popp
Max Reger Institut, Bonn
January 1993

PREFACE

Ever since the musical world acquainted itself with the compositions of a rustic Bavarian named Max Reger, who today is often remembered more for his sarcastic humour than for his works, the music of this unique composer has been highly controversial. The response of musicians, critics, and musically educated audiences has been and still is rather ambiguous, vacillating between the utmost extremes of enthusiastic acceptance and vociferous rejection, the latter being replaced today by a kind of benign indifference. This is especially true in North America—an interesting phenomenon, given that Max Reger's music over the years has become reasonably well entrenched in the consciousness of European musicians and audiences. A succinct analysis of this situation is provided by William E. Grim in his *Bio-Bibliography* of Max Reger:

> ...outside of Germany, Reger remains largely an unknown composer who is often the subject of denigrating comments by musicians and musicologists, many of whom have never heard a single composition by Reger. This phenomenon is somewhat curious in that with the exception of his Munich period...Reger's works were generally met with approval and critical acclaim. At the time of his death, Reger was

internationally acknowledged as a master composer, and memorial concerts occurred throughout the world, even in Russia which was at war with Germany at that time.[1]

Although Max Reger has become established internationally as a composer of organ music through his substantial works in this genre, his piano music is hardly ever performed and, one could even say, is basically unknown, some exceptions not withstanding. In contemplating the particular lack of interest in Reger's rather prolific output for piano, one concludes that there indeed might be a salient reason for this puzzling situation.

It is well known that Johannes Brahms was extremely critical with respect to his musical creations, occasionally even asking Clara Schumann or Joseph Joachim for advice pertinent to his compositional endeavours. Towards the end of his life he found it necessary to destroy quite a number of compositions in a kind of final musical *auto-da-fé*. We have no direct proof that Max Reger took such drastic action, although he once mentioned in a letter to his publisher that he was "destroying enough material that is not satisfactory to me."[2]

Reger composed with tremendous ease, feeding a wide array of publishers who expected to receive nearly every composition fresh from his desk for immediate publication. He admittedly did not always invest the utmost scrutiny and necessary care into the compositional process, particularly in his earlier pieces for piano. Reger himself at one point declared a number of these works "hopeless nonsense."[3] It is unfortunate that—aside from being unduly ubiquitous—his whole output for solo piano appears somewhat unbalanced in its overall compositional quality.

The aim of this publication is therefore to help the ever-exploring pianist and the interested student of piano music to find their way to the high-quality core of Max Reger's piano music without having to undertake the time-consuming task of separating the wheat from the chaff. Among the many works for solo piano Max Reger produced during his very active life, quite a number reveal imbalances or weaknesses of one kind or another. Some pieces show the master still in his formative stages, during which he was seeking to amalgamate his own idiosyncratic language with the inherent possibilities of the piano as a medium of expression; others are strongly reminiscent of stylistic traits of other composers without yet arriving at a readily identifiable Regerian idiom. In addition, Max Reger's attempts in some of his more overblown creations to eliminate or transform certain stylistic features that were considered by his contemporaries to be worn-out, stereotypic compositional elements were only occasionally successful.

On the positive side, we find interspersed some astonishing creations that show Max Reger at his best, amalgamating a multitude of imaginative musical ideas with an incredible compositional mastery, expressed in bold harmonic concepts and overpowering logical polyphonic structures. Among those compositions are impressive pianistic masterpieces immensely suitable for public performance, such as the *Telemann Variations*, op. 134. A considerable number of highly imaginative character pieces offer themselves as extremely useful tools in the teaching process. Their intrinsic pedagogical value manifests itself especially in Max Reger's fusion of compositional techniques derived from the baroque era with chromatically extended harmonic procedures, thereby expanding the idiosyncrasies of romantic expressiveness. In addition, Max Reger's oeuvre for solo piano contains a number of compositions of the so-called "humoresque type," mainly represented by pieces with titles like *Burleske*, *Humoreske*, *Burletta*, and, to some extent, *Capriccio*. Through a number of original figurative formulas Max Reger has made unique and lasting contributions to this particular genre.

After presenting a short biographical survey, it seems therefore logical to draw attention to those works for solo piano which

(1) show Reger at his best in his most original creations in this genre,

(2) are rewarding concert pieces, and

(3) have substantial pedagogical value with respect to his idiosyncratic polyphonic writing, unique harmonic language, and characteristic figurative patterns.

The discussion focuses on the practical, interpretive aspects of Reger's works for solo piano. It touches on theoretical analysis only in so far as is necessary to describe Reger's style in general, although it is important to draw special attention to a number of specific stylistic and compositional features central to his musical language. An understanding of those features is of course essential for any performer or teacher who wants to attain more than a superficial familiarity with Max Reger's idiom.

ACKNOWLEDGEMENTS

The creation of this book was not possible without ample support by many individuals. I am deeply obliged to Drs. Susanne Popp and Susanne Shigihara of the Max Reger Institut, Bonn, Germany, for special assistance in the research process. I am also indebted to Drs. William Kinderman and Gerhard Wuensch for their valuable advice, to Dr. Garret Epp and Judith Johnson for their expertise in revising the final draft of the book and to my dedicated research assistants Corinne Cherry and in particular Roger Admiral. It goes without saying that I am extremely grateful to Norma Gutteridge, director of the University of Alberta Press, Mary Mahoney-Robson and Kerry Watt for their unwavering enthusiasm in the publishing process.

The cooperation of the publishing firm Breitkopf and Härtel, Wiesbaden, Germany, allowing me to use the Max Reger Gesamtausgabe for most of the 145 examples, is highly appreciated and gratefully acknowledged. I am also deeply indebted to the publishing firm G. Henle Verlag, München, for the permission to use the Henle Urtext Edition for the following examples: 8, 9, 14, 17, 51–56, 62, 67, 102–109, 125 and 136b.

1

THE EPIGONAL REVOLUTIONARY

Max Reger (1873–1916) was one of the most controversial German composers of the late romantic period. He was born into a time that was politically and sociologically determined by an unusually long period of peace among Europe's main political forces, a time that fostered the belief that the human species could be conditioned to control and master all problems, be they political, economic, or social, if only goodwill prevailed and the unlimited ingenuity of the *homo sapiens* could be brought to fruition. A general complacency was spreading throughout the populace and was also rampant among the political leaders of the day, who seemed to be convinced that an apparently secure balance of power in Europe would prevent any future military clashes.

In that particular climate of hope around the turn of the century a sometimes supercilious self-confidence skidded dangerously close to a peculiar arrogance that could even be interpreted as a spiritual megalomania. However, artists in general did not identify with this attitude, and were extending their antennas towards the future. They perceived an era of imminent revolutionary changes and increasingly expressed themselves in new, equally revolutionary, artistic creations. In music in particular, highly sensitive artists found the sometimes overwhelmingly sentimental style of the then common "genre composer" unbearable, passé, and far from the essential honesty and clarity they strove to attain.

They envisaged a powerful new musical language that would expand, transcend, or replace ways of expression they found epigonal, stale, and unimaginative. The hypertrophy of romanticism was antithetical to the new evolving styles, which included Impressionism with Claude Debussy and Neo-Classicism with Igor Stravinsky, as well as the expansion of the harmonic language by Béla Bartók and the dodecaphonic system of Arnold Schönberg.

In this context it is worth noting that Schönberg and those composers who in the early twenties gathered under the umbrella of the Verein für musikalische Privataufführungen in Wien und Prag were originally very fond of Reger's bold harmonic procedures and claimed him as one of their own. As a matter of fact, in the programs of their concerts, works by Max Reger could be found more frequently than those by any other composer.

While we today think of Max Reger as a representative of the late romantic era, we should not forget that around the turn of the century he was considered by many of his contemporaries to be an extreme revolutionary, in particular with respect to his treatment of harmony. The enmity he encountered was immense, especially during his so-called "Munich Period" (1901–1907). Reger strongly believed that the expansion of the tonal language had to be an evolutionary rather than a revolutionary process, thereby maintaining traditional forms and procedures. In one of his letters to Adalbert Lindner he portrayed himself as an ardent admirer of Bach, Beethoven, and Brahms and expressed surprise that he was seen as someone preaching revolution. On the contrary, he considered himself working towards a further development of their particular styles.[1] In this his basic aims were similar to those of Johannes Brahms, the composer he revered most after Johann Sebastian Bach. Helmut Wirth's discerning remark that Reger's love for Bach "went through the prism of Brahms" shows a deep understanding of this matter.[2]

Reger considered himself the torch-bearer of those "absolute" musicians who honoured and maintained the traditional forms and compositional procedures established by the great masters of the baroque and classical eras. Thus he immediately found himself in opposition to the Neudeutsche Schule of Wagner and Liszt, with its programmatic ideas which evolved as

Program of a concert of the
Verein für musikalische Pri-
vataufführungen in Prag
1920, featuring Reger's last
Violin Sonata op. 139.
(Courtesy of The Arnold
Schoenberg Institute
Archives, Los Angeles, Cali-
fornia)

KONZERTDIREKTION Dr. W. ZEMÁNEK.

MOZARTEUM.

Sonntag, den 7. März 1920 um ¹⁄₂8 abend.

I. KONZERT

des Vereines für musikalische Privataufführungen in Wien.

Leitung: ARNOLD SCHÖNBERG.

✶

VORTRAGSFOLGE:

MAX REGER: Sonate für Violine u. Klavier C-moll op. 139.
Con passione — Largo — Vivace — Andantino con variazioni.
Violine: **Rudolf Kolisch.** Klavier: **Dr. Ernst Bachrich.**

JOSEF SUK: ›Erlebtes und Erträumtes‹. 10 Klavierstücke.
1. Mit Humor und ironisch, stellenweise grimmig erregt.
2. Unruhig, schüchtern, nicht allzu ausdrucksvoll.
3. Geheimnisvoll und sehr duftig.
4. In sich versunken, später mit gesteigerter Energie.
5. Zur Genesung meines Sohnes.
6. Still vergnügt — sehnsüchtig und träumerisch.
7. Schlicht, später mit bezwingender Macht.
8. Fein und geschwätzig.
9. Lispelnd und geheimnisvoll
10. Den vergessenen Grabhügeln auf unserem Dorffriedhof.

RUDOLF SERKIN.

CLAUDE DEBUSSY: En blanc et noir. Trois morceaux pour 2 pianos à 4 mains (1915).

I.	II.
Qui reste à sa place	Prince porté soit des serfs Eolus
Et ne danse pas	En la forest ou domine Glaucus.
De quelque disgrâce	Ou privé soit de paix et d'espérance
Fait l'aveu tout bas.	Car digne n'est de posséder vertus
	Qui mal vouldroit au royaume de France.
(J. Barbier et M. Carré — ›Romeo et Juliette‹.)	(François Villon — ›Ballade contre les ennemies de la France‹ [envoi]).

III.
Vver, vous n'est qu'un vilain . . . .
(Charles d'Orléans.)

Eduard Steuermann u. Rudolf Serkin.

☛ **Es wird gebeten, Beifall oder Mißfallen erst am Schluße des Konzertes zu äußern.** ☚

Das II. Konzert findet Montag, den 8. März um ¹⁄₂8 abend im Mozarteum statt.

PREIS K 1·—.

the generally accepted principles of compositional direction in his time. Max Reger clearly delineated his identification with "absolute music" in a letter to the singer Joseph Loritz, in which he insisted that he could not "sail along" with the "deluge of programmatic music."[3]

Seen from our present historical distance, Max Reger's musical development appears to have been a logical process which was determined by his innate musical talent, strong influences of other composers, and his very distinct personal traits, an aspect which should not be underestimated. However, these traits should not be allowed to dominate the discussion of the music itself, as they often have. Rather, Max Reger's personal excesses and characteristic ambiguities should be evaluated in an objective, balanced way. As pointed out in the recent edition of *The New Oxford Companion to Music*,

> [Max Reger is] poorly accepted outside his native Germany; but the stereotyped image of him as a drunkard and a turgid contrapuntist is now loosing currency.[4]

Likewise, as Ernst Brennecke has stated,

> this man was neither God nor insect, as he is alternately painted, but a fascinating personality possessing both god-like and spiderish attributes: a combination of amazing strength and equally amazing weaknesses, of charm and repulsiveness, for which a nervous age like the present should really make some show of interest, and perhaps of gratitude.[5]

Reger's creative impulses often vacillated as much as his personality. One extremely important facet of this unique personality was a strong susceptibility to any type of stimulus, which can also be interpreted as a form of super-sensitivity. From the psychological point of view it is obvious that such an impressionable and therefore vulnerable personality must have felt itself to be in constant need of some kind of protection. This need manifested itself in various ways, among which the most positive might have been Reger's determination to convince the world that he as a person and composer had something very important in store for it, since this proved to be such a tremendous impetus for his artistic productivity.

We know, of course, that the unique personality of a composer and the influence of certain circumstances may reveal themselves in various degrees in the general characteristics of the creative process. Mozart and Beethoven could be mentioned as two very contrasting examples, the former relatively independent of inner and outer influences, the latter frequently influenced and moulded by the vicissitudes and conditions of life in general.

Max Reger certainly falls into the category of composers whose general oeuvre and even specific works seem to mirror in a definable way some of the personal idiosyncrasies, specific events, and given circumstances that influenced their feeling and thinking. It is obvious, for example, that one of Reger's character traits, best paraphrased as a kind of "emotional duality" in which he oscillated widely between his proverbial, aggressive humour and deeply felt loving sentiment, found a commensurate expression in his music.

All composers, of course, respond more or less to specific stimuli related to their work. One could mention commissions received (such as those from Count Razumovsky resulting in Beethoven's *Razumovsky Quartets*), intense relationships with fellow musicians (such as the excellent clarinetist Richard Mühlfeld who inspired Brahms's *Clarinet Sonatas*, op. 120, and his *Clarinet Trio*, op. 114), poetry (such as poems by Johann Wolfgang von Goethe or Friedrich Wilhelm Müller, without which certain songs by Schubert would not exist), or for that matter any libretto as the initial impulse for the composition of an opera, to cite only a few examples.

Max Reger's overabundance of musical ideas and his tremendous mastery of the compositional process were powerful assets ready to be put into action at any given time. This was even recognized by his strongest critic, Dr. Rudolf Louis, who acknowledged Max Reger's "stupendous compositional skills, the unfathomable richness of his contrapuntal combinations, and his power of invention with respect to new and unheard-of harmonic progressions."[6] In a sense, his way of composing is similar to that of Mozart: the musical creation seems to have been totally finalized in his mind in such a way that its materialization on paper often was just the transcription of an existing entity. It is well documented that this process was a continuous one without any respite whatsoever, a fountain from which during Reger's relatively short life a seemingly endless phalanx of compositions gushed forth. This fact is mentioned whenever Reger's compositional output is discussed. Oswald Kühn contemplates a possibly interesting correlation between Reger's "unusual or even frightening" productivity and the fact that everything composed was also published immediately.[7]

The 146 opus numbers are certainly indicative of an incessant creativity. Among piano works they include not only very extended compositions such as the *Bach Variations*, op. 81, but also many shorter pieces, mostly grouped under one opus number, such as *Aus meinem Tagebuch*, op. 82, comprising four volumes with a total of 35 pieces. In addition, Max Reger produced an unusually large number of transcriptions, including an arrangement for two pianos of his own *Mozart Variations*, op. 132. His transcriptions of other composers' works ranged from those of Johann Sebastian Bach to those of Hugo Wolf.

With the exception of the opera and specific creations for the ballet, Max Reger employed all the musical genres a serious composer of "absolute music" would consider common vehicles for musical expression at that time. This included music for keyboard (organ and piano) and orchestral instruments (violin, viola, violoncello, flute, and clarinet) and orchestra and solo instrument with orchestra, as well as chamber music, choral works, and songs.

Most of the works for solo piano to be discussed here are in the form of the character piece, in its basic A–B–A form, with B generally providing a strong contrast. The choice of this form certainly was commensurate with the general acceptance of the character piece at that time, the best examples of which are among the *Intermezzi* by Johannes Brahms. Nearly all of these works are found in collections comprising from 5 to 35 pieces under one opus number. The sonata in its traditional form, although declining in importance, had still been an important vehicle of musical expression in the romantic era, as demonstrated by Chopin and Brahms. It is conspicuously absent in Reger's solo piano music, except in its smaller version, the sonatina. However, it is very much present in his chamber music.

As a unique and distinct contrast to the numerous shorter pieces, the gigantic Bach and Telemann variations (op. 81 and op. 134) are compositional highlights in Max Reger's piano oeuvre. These are monumental works, which certainly deserve to be placed with the great variation works of Schumann (*Études Symphoniques*, op. 13), Brahms (*Handel Variations*, op. 24), and even Beethoven (*Diabelli Variations*, op. 120). Whatever specific reservations one might have about Max Reger's general style and expression, one has to admit that the massive *Bach Variations* alone would have secured him immortality as a composer. In Reger's time it was not at all unusual for a music critic to appraise his art of variation as being comparable to that of the greatest masters in this genre.[8]

It goes without saying that the music of a controversial composer like Max Reger will be understood better if some personal information precedes any further discussion of his work. A thorough, detailed biographical account is beyond the scope of this inquiry. Among various comprehensive biographies available, the one by Max Reger's closest friend, Fritz Stein (1879–1961), still seems the most authoritative.[9]

However, since Max Reger was in a strikingly intense way reacting to various stimuli, whether these originated in his own complex personality, in his overall environment, or specifically in the world of musical composition—an especially volatile world around 1900—some of the most germane facets of his character and life should be mentioned before an attempt is made to discuss his music in general and the piano compositions in particular.

2

A TUMULTUOUS LIFE

Shortly after the birth of Max Reger in 1873 in Brand, a small village in northern Bavaria, the Reger family moved to Weiden, a larger town in the same region, where Max's father Joseph received an appointment at a training school for teachers. At that time the preparation of teachers was considered an important task within the *Königreich Bayern* and the position of a *Seminarlehrer* carried considerable status. Joseph Reger was greatly interested in music himself—he wrote a book on harmony and assembled a house-organ for his and subsequently his son's use—and so the talented young "Maxl" was assured an early exposure to good music, the more so since he began taking piano lessons from his mother Philomena when he was five years old. It might be of interest to know that in the *Realschule* the boy showed a strong talent for mathematics—an aptitude obviously conducive to his later phenomenal combinatory mastery in the field of counterpoint.

It augured well when Adalbert Lindner (1860–1946), teacher and organist in Weiden, took over Reger's musical guidance in 1884. Under the significant musical influence exerted by his new mentor during the next five years, Max Reger studied piano literature from Bach to Brahms and acquainted himself through four-hand piano reductions with important orchestral and operatic works of the classical and romantic periods, including those of Liszt and Wagner. He became interested in the organ and began intensive studies of harmony and counterpoint.

In 1888 Reger took the opportunity to hear Wagner's operas *Parsifal* and *Meistersinger* in Bayreuth. If one imagines that this was his first chance to hear a full orchestra within an operatic context, one can understand that the impressionable 15-year-old was overwhelmed and deeply moved. He decided to become a musician, documenting this desire with a major composition, an "*ouverture*" in B minor scored for flute, clarinet, piano, and strings and comprising some 120 pages! The sheer magnitude of this work seems symptomatic of the well documented rustic buoyancy of Reger's personality, which neither in personal nor in artistic utterances was free of excesses. In addition, Max Reger—like Beethoven—was clearly conscious of his talent, and convinced that he had a mission to fulfill in the musical world. It soon became obvious that his *cause célèbre* throughout his life was to be the defence of "absolute music" against the onslaught of "program music." In a letter to Georg Stern in 1910 he deplored the denigration of the richest forms of musical art like the fugue and the passacaglia, and even predicted the eventual dissipation of the "aberrant fog" of the symphonic poem.[1]

As mentioned before, Reger seemed always to have been extremely vulnerable and easily hurt, and thus he frequently overreacted to criticism. In his thoughtful analysis of Reger's psychological problems, Rainer Cadenbach characterizes this sensitivity and consequently often "uncontrolled, aggressive behaviour" as a result of his deeply rooted envy of presumed competitors based on a "boundless insecurity regarding his own works."[2] Others have interpreted Reger's sometimes sarcastic and offensive verbal utterances facetiously as the natural idiosyncratic expressiveness of the Bavarian people. Whether valid or not, such a judgement is not important within this context. The fact is that Max Reger's frequently derisive outspokenness created as many enemies as his sensitive, loving attitude towards those he considered his supporters resulted in deep, long-lasting friendships. And in his belligerent way he quite often recruited his friends to his battle camp, from which he agitated with amazing aggression against his real or perceived foes, as revealed by quite a number of his letters. At one time he even went to the extreme of mentioning revenge for the time in which society "had declared me musically perverse with impunity," and of "musical killing" as a form of thorough retribution.[3]

As documented in his substantial book,[4] Adalbert Lindner recognized the tremendous musical talent of his student and had the aforementioned overture sent to Hugo Riemann (1849–1919), who showed a keen interest in the young man and exerted probably the most decisive influence on his artistic development in the following years. Max Reger began structured musical studies under Riemann at the conservatory in Sondershausen in 1890. When his teacher moved to Wiesbaden, he followed and continued his studies at the Fuchs'sche Konservatorium. Riemann was a towering personality in the general musical scene in Germany and beyond, and made lasting contributions to music theory and related fields. He is known foremost through his important *Musik-Lexikon*,[5] his salient publications on numerous aspects of musical analysis, and his characteristic system of analysis related mainly to the masterworks of Bach, Beethoven, and Brahms. He thereby established a value system that was widely accepted in his time, and strongly influenced Reger at the beginning of his career. Later in his life, however, Reger liberated himself from the constrictions of Riemann's system, as he perceived them.

In this context it might be quite revealing not only to study the compositional craftsmanship in Reger's music, but also to take note of his *Beiträge zur Modulationslehre*,[6] a publication that sold well but also caused some biting criticism. In particular, Heinrich Schenker's comments in his diary deriding this publication as an "inexcusable booklet, narrow-minded, crazy, self-complacent and childish" were typical of some of the negative reactions at that time.[7] As was to be expected, Reger feverishly defended his publication in two subsequent articles.[8]

Max Reger's time in Wiesbaden, which came to an abrupt end in 1898, was artistically fruitful yet devastating in personal terms. His progress as an artist in general had been phenomenal and his compositional activities prolific and substantial, encompassing chamber music, works for organ and piano, songs, and arrangements, mainly of works by Bach. His success even radiated to Berlin, then the undisputed cultural centre of Germany, where the first "All Reger Concert" took place in 1894.[9] Subsequent contacts with Brahms, D'Albert, and Busoni were extremely stimulating and helped to shape a more universal outlook than was encountered in the sometimes narrow academic realm of Hugo Riemann's circle. The exchange of letters with Ferruccio Busoni, who later, after a concert in Berlin in January 1905, hailed him as the "greatest living and deeply German composer,"[10] was especially encouraging.

However, the temptations of a free student life included rather strong excesses in tobacco and alcohol, as indicated in a typical pun by Max Reger himself, who called this particular period of his life "Meine Sturm und Tranck Zeit."[11] It resulted in a physical and mental collapse, which forced Reger to return to Weiden to recover under the loving care of his family.

Max Reger's mental situation had been so precarious that his mother even contemplated the possibility of her son entering a psychiatric institution. It is therefore the more surprising that after his return to Weiden, Reger very soon set himself a strict daily working schedule as a freelance composer. Within the next three years he established a substantial reputation as a composer through some of his most important works for organ and thrust himself into the centre of the controversy over compositional styles that was then raging. The opinions of enthusiastic followers like Fritz Stein (1879–1961) and Thomas-Cantor Karl Straube (1873–1950), who premiered nearly all of Reger's organ compositions, were often outweighed by those of sceptical critics and outright opponents.

Although he usually wrote in a rather objective and responsible manner, the most important music critic in Munich of the period, Dr. Rudolf Louis (1870–1914), was generally opposed to Max Reger's music. The opinion was even voiced that as a consequence of Louis's strong enmity, Reger was generally ignored for many years.[12] The growing controversy also included Hugo Riemann, whose comments about his former student became increasingly negative. Max Reger's personality seemed to thrive under these circumstances, especially after the whole family moved in 1901 to Munich, at that time an important centre of the Neudeutsche Schule, then perceived as the epitome of musical progress. The most important local representatives of this camp were Max von Schillings (1868–1933), Ludwig Thuille (1861–1907), and their students, who evolved as vociferous antagonists to Max Reger and created belligerent situations not only in words, but also in occasional personal clashes. However, Max Reger's students were equally belligerent, if not more so. After Rudolf Louis's devastatingly negative review of the *Sinfonietta* in Munich in 1906, for instance, Reger's students (the "*Schwefelbande*") presented a noisy "*Katzenmusik*" in front of the critic's home. Louis's subsequent ironic retort in the form of a polite statement of thanks to the students published in the *Münchner Neueste Nachrichten* did not advance Max Reger's case.[13]

By that time Reger had established himself as his own best interpreter, mainly as a pianist, in which capacity even the most vicious critics accepted him without question. There is no doubt that Reger was propagandizing his own works with an insistence bordering on fanaticism. It is difficult to believe that a human being could endure the kind of pace Reger subjected himself to in his concert itineraries—travelling from one city to the next, frequently during the night, rehearsing shortly before the concert, performing in the evening, often with local musicians, and taking the night train to the next destination. According to his own account, he frequently created his next composition in his mind in the relative seclusion of railway compartments, postponing writing it down to a more suitable time.

On these concert tours Max Reger performed as a pianist in his chamber music and duo piano works, accompanied singers in his songs, and sometimes played works by other composers. It is interesting that he relatively seldom performed his own solo piano works and then only a few selected shorter pieces. The most weighty and frequently performed numbers in his programs were the two gigantic works for two pianos, the *Beethoven Variations*, op. 86 (1904), and the *Introduktion, Passacaglia, und Fuge*, op. 96 (1906), for which he often teamed up with a local pianist, usually having only one rehearsal shortly before the concert.

Numerous comments have been made pertaining to Reger's innate pianistic talent and the dynamic flexibility in his piano playing, in particular with respect to his unique *pianissimo* and his uncanny ability to colour the sound. These are obvious in the few recordings that are available. Adalbert Lindner, for instance, referred to Max Reger as the "born motor talent . . . with an eminent gift to recognize a musical context and transfer it to the hands with lightning speed."[14] A comment by Hermann Poppen, according to whom "each large crescendo was taken by storm with a forward-surging tempo, each subsiding diminuendo calmed the pace again,"[15] is indicative of an important horizontal flexibility in Max Reger's own playing. Although he must have had an exact knowledge of the idiosyncrasies

A postcard to Henriette Schelle, dated April 5, 1905, graphically reveals the intensity with which Reger tried to promote the performance of op. 81. (Max Reger Institut)

"Meine Dame, unterlassen Sie das Lachen, das stört mich im Spiel." ("My lady, please refrain from laughing. It is disturbing my playing.") *Reger am Klavier*, 1913, by Wilhelm Thielmann. (Max Reger Institut)

of the piano,[16] one can safely surmise that Reger's mastery of the instrument was based more on intuition than on conscious practice and therefore had a highly personalized expressiveness, which fascinated his audiences.

The pianist Hugo Jinkertz (1878–1943), who once called Max Reger a "piano-playing genius," appeared relatively often as a partner in his concerts. His own account of Max Reger's interpretative style is thus presumably reliable.[17] He mentions, for example, that Reger, in performing a piano concerto by J.S. Bach, added additional voices and octave doublings on the spur of the moment, following his spontaneous, brilliant inspiration.[18] This, of course, is characteristic of the idiosyncratic performance style of the romantic epoch, a tradition which our modern, sometimes excessively purist, attitude no longer condones. Jinkertz also mentions that in his later years Max Reger as pianist could not live up to the technical demands of his great solo works, especially the *Bach Variations*, op. 81, and the *Klavierkonzert*, op. 114.[19]

As a composer who was expanding his compositional activities into nearly every possible medium, Max Reger also promoted and defended his musical and philosophical beliefs in a number of pertinent publications.[20] These offer additional insight into the psychological framework of a man who incessantly tried to influence those not yet convinced of his musical language and who often reported triumphantly to his friends on any perceived victory for "his side." Still, Max Reger had high ideals for himself and his music, as is obvious from a moving statement found in one of his letters, in which he mentions art and religion as "the highest and only means" of liberating human beings from the material world, and deplores the decline of humaneness in the arts.[21]

His growing recognition, his marriage to Elsa von Bercken (born von Bagenski) in 1902, and a lifetime contract with the Leipzig publishing firm of Lauterbach & Kuhn in 1903 strengthened Reger's self-confidence and seemed to embolden the composer to write some of his most complex and controversial works, including the *Violinsonate*, op. 72, which can be considered the epitome of the "Wild Munich Period." The polarization of the interested public was complete. On the negative side, a number of critical comments were openly hostile and derisive. A small sample reveals devastating verdicts ranging from (1) "no inner musical content," (2) "extreme artificiality," (3) "deliberate mannerism," (4) "desert of monotony," and (5) "rhythmical sterility" to (6) "sick, perverse music" and (7) "apotheosis of musical ugliness."[22]

It seems that after all those and similar invectives had saturated the critical climate surrounding Reger's music, more and more positive comments began to appear, and the balance of the critical scale began to move slowly but continuously towards sometimes enthusiastic acceptance. In spite of this adversity, or perhaps because of it, Max Reger continued his meteoric ascent. Being the "hottest item on the market" seemed to give him considerable satisfaction. Finally, the *Bach Variations*, op. 81 (1904), for solo piano, the *Beethoven Variations*, op. 86 (1904), and the *Introduktion, Passacaglia, und Fuge*, op. 96 (1906), for two pianos cemented his position

Max and Elsa Reger in their first apartment in Leipzig, 1910. Photograph from Hoenisch, Leipzig. (Max Reger Institut)

among the acknowledged voices of a revolutionary era in the development of musical styles.

In 1907 Max Reger was appointed *Universitätsmusikdirektor* and accepted a position as theory teacher at the renowned conservatory in Leipzig, a city which in the beginning of the twentieth century was one of the most important musical centres in Germany. With respect to his teaching activities and the enthusiastic response of many talented students, these short years in Leipzig were probably the most fulfilling and satisfying in Reger's life. Quite a number of outstanding students[23] gathered around him, eagerly absorbing the revered composer's compositional credos, which he reportedly transmitted in a very systematic way. As a composer Max Reger now concentrated more and more on larger orchestral works, without interrupting a nearly continuous stream of chamber music pieces. His famous *Variationen und Fuge über ein Thema von J.A. Hiller*, op. 100 (1907), and his *100th Psalm*, op. 106 (1908/09), for choir, orchestra, and organ, were examples of this new trend. Incidentally, the first part of the *100th Psalm* was composed as a musical tribute for a *doctor honoris causa* bestowed upon him by the University of Jena. Having received quite a number of important official honours, Max Reger was on the one hand attracted to and proud of them, while on the other he often scoffed at them in his usual humorous way. However, there are strong indications that he actively solicited honours and titles. More recent studies have drawn attention to the psychologically important correlation of Reger's inner insecurity and his compensatory need to be acknowledged by the public and the intellectual elite.[24]

Given Reger's outspoken personality and his extreme sensitivity to criticism, it was predictable that Leipzig too was only a temporary artistic home for him. In 1911 he grasped the opportunity of an appointment as Hofkapellmeister in Meiningen under the generous sponsorship of Duke Georg, who was proud of and financially generous to "his" orchestra. This was a prestigious post, primarily since Hans von Bülow and Fritz Steinbach had infused this orchestra with superb artistry, which had suffered to a certain extent under Reger's immediate predecessor, Wilhelm Berger. The orchestra was highly regarded and travelled extensively in Germany, as well as to adjacent countries. For Reger, these concerts were thus a fitting venue in which to promote his own works. In addition, he still retained his position as a teacher of composition at the conservatory in Leipzig, and also maintained his usual hectic concert schedule in spite of several sincere but unsuccessful attempts to curtail his incessant activities. During the 1912/13 season alone, Reger performed in 106 concerts, either conducting or performing as a pianist. The number of substantial works created in that "Meiningen Period," including the *Konzert im Alten Stil*, op. 123, the *Römischer Triumphgesang*, op. 126, and the *Ballet-Suite*, op. 130, is absolutely astonishing. It seemed as if a mighty geyser of imagination were constantly welling within the master, pressing forward with an inexorable force to be manifested in ever new musical creations.

Yet the first definite signs of total exhaustion could no longer be ignored; Max Reger had neglected his health for too long. The sometimes excessive consumption of alcoholic beverages certainly contributed to the sudden decline of his life force. After a total breakdown on February 28, 1914, with a subsequent recuperation period of only four weeks, the composer relinquished his post in Meiningen, but soon was exploding with new compositional ideas, among them the popular *Variationen und Fuge über ein Thema von W.A. Mozart*, op. 132, based on the first movement of the piano sonata in A major, K.331, and—most important for pianists— the *Variationen und Fuge über ein Thema von G.Ph. Telemann*, op. 134. This work constitutes his last major composition for solo piano, although a collection of highly imaginative character pieces under the title *Träume am Kamin*, op. 143, was still to follow.

With his wife Elsa and his two adopted daughters Christa and Lotti, Max Reger moved to Jena, where he had bought a respectable villa. Hopeful that the inspiring environment of this university town would help to focus his diffuse life not only physically, but also spiritually, he was talking about the "beginning of the free Jena style."[25] The *Violinsonate*, op. 139 (1914/15), and the *Klarinetten Quintett,* op. 146 (1915/16), are usually cited as examples of a notable stylistic refinement in Reger's later compositions.

For those friends and admirers who intimately knew Max Reger and the many extremes that marked his life, the news of his death after a heart attack at the age of 43 came as no particular surprise. When he was found dead in his bed in the Hotel Hentschel in Leipzig on May 11, 1916, the first page of the proofs of his *Acht Geistliche Gesänge*, op. 138, was lying open, revealing the text, "Der Mensch lebt und bestehet nur eine kleine Zeit." ("Man lives and exists only a short time.") The master certainly had been aware of this truth, as one of his earlier remarks revealed his conviction that he would not live much longer. The symbolic meaning of his last major *a capella* work lying open beside his deathbed can be interpreted as a sign of Max Reger's belief that one must not squander even a minute of one's precious life, that all available energy must be directed towards the fulfilment of one's destiny regardless of the price exacted by such extreme demands. Reger's substantial legacy as a composer would seem to justify such a sacrifice.

3

A STYLISTIC ENIGMA

Viel' Feind', viel Ehr' (many enemies, much honour)—this old German maxim could well characterize Max Reger's situation as a composer in his time. As already mentioned, strong camps of indiscriminate adulation on one side and degrading condemnation on the other had developed quite early in his career. Even today, pockets of polarization still prevail, albeit expressed in more objective and less emotional terms.[1]

It is somewhat ironic that important stylistic features which were perceived and criticized by a number of Reger's contemporaries as being outrageously revolutionary are in our times equally censured as being epigonal in form and substance. Indeed, in hindsight they appear rather old-fashioned and are in no way linked to the progressive language of modern music already strongly emerging during Reger's lifetime. However, we should not forget that Arnold Schönberg had a very positive attitude towards Reger and promoted his music in the concerts of the *Verein für musikalische Privataufführungen* in Vienna.

With all this in mind, one is well advised to try to judge single characteristics not so much in comparison with the works of others, but within the framework of the totality of the composer's own work, just as we today accept Schubert's piano sonatas not as being written in the style of

Beethoven, but as existing quite clearly in their own right. Thus it seems only fair first to delineate the most obvious stylistic features of Max Reger's piano music without making any value judgement, although it might be elucidating to quote some of the stronger reactions they have elicited.

It is widely accepted that Reger's concentrated polyphonic style, his often irrational metric proportions, his asymmetrical phrase structures, his massive sound spectra, and his expansive harmonic concepts are his most characteristic compositional stylistic elements, and also his most controversial. In particular, his unique harmonic language with its inherent ambiguity as to the functional value and meaning of chordal progressions has stirred up both admiration and criticism. By veiling or weakening tonal centres, Reger frequently creates the impression of a floating harmonic instability, which some analysts have associated with the term "musical prose," as opposed to the established logic of traditional chord progressions with clear delineations of cadential incises as a means of establishing structure.[2] Cadenbach mentions that on the basis of evidence seen in his sketches, Reger seemed to have been interested mainly in "the sound characteristics of the individual chords as such and not in their correlation as to grammar and syntax."[3] Reger himself was quite conscious of the impact his harmonic procedures had on his contemporaries, and defended them vigorously with terms like "only seemingly willful, but absolutely logical."[4]

In this context one should not forget that Reger's substantial oeuvre for organ, with its massive harmonic structures and grand dimensions, was accepted quite readily by artists and the public alike and is today considered an essential part of the organist's repertoire. Neither Reger's piano music nor his extensive output in the field of chamber music, nor for that matter any other works within his prolific oeuvre, have had the same general world-wide acceptance, notwithstanding the relative popularity of the *Mozart Variations*, op. 132, for orchestra. This might be symptomatic in the sense that the dense texture and hypertrophic musical structure of Reger's music could be seen in a kind of symbiotic relationship with the organ, the unique sound spectrum of which seems to accommodate these specific Regerian sonorities better than any other instrument.

If one sees Reger's compositional procedures as organic in the sense of propagating a constantly evolving stream of musical thoughts and thereby creating its own idiosyncratic forms, one must accept the resulting musical language as valid and autonomous, and judge it accordingly. The eminent music critic Alexander Berrsche speaks of music "growing in a natural way from one [musical] state into another."[5] However, if one accepts the premise of everlasting objective musical laws, such as those defined by Reger's teacher and mentor Hugo Riemann and expressed in his many important publications, one has to agree with Riemann's criticism of Reger's complicated textures, overloaded "technical apparatus," and intentionally daring harmonic and modulatory procedures, and with his characterization of Reger's expansive richness as disturbing, stereotypical mannerism.[6]

Examples of Reger's chromatically expanded harmonic procedures abound throughout his expansive oeuvre. Note, for instance, the following:

EXAMPLE 1. *Bach Variations*, op. 81, m. 49

A detailed discussion of Reger's harmonic concepts in general would be far beyond the scope of this publication and unnecessary in view of the many excellent studies on this topic, in particular the one by Gerd Sievers.[7] Attention should be drawn, however, to the bold cadential steps, frequently occurring at the end of compositions, that were considered unconventional in Reger's time, in particular those based on subdominant-tonic functions or progressions based on specific modes such as Dorian or Phrygian. Quite often we find the modulatory device of the Neapolitan sixth employed as a means to establish the final delineation of the tonality.

EXAMPLE 2.   *Aus meinem Tagebuch*, op. 82/I, no. 10, mm. 39–42

It seems that Reger had some problems in transforming his incredible creativity, his overabundance of musical ideas, and his powerful combinatory skills or, as some might say, ability to manipulate musical material, into immediately recognizable and understandable musical structures—recognizable and understandable not only by the experts, but also by the music-loving public in general. Carl Dahlhaus was aware of this problem and published an article on the obvious difficulty of understanding Reger's music. He specifically points to fast harmony changes that "demand a non-functional colouristic aural perception" which, however, "is hindered by the austere character of the music. . . ." Consequently one seems to be called upon to "recreate assiduously the musical logic," an impossible task since "the rapid harmonic events are too precipitous."[8]

However, Max Reger was very conscious of his artistic aims. He knew exactly what he wanted and tried to be as explicit as possible, especially in his meticulous notation. An excerpt from the *Bach Variations*, op. 81, in which Reger with admirable ingenuity graphically delineates meaningful groupings and intricate rhythmic proportions, might serve as an example.

EXAMPLE 3.   *Bach Variations*, op. 81, m. 50

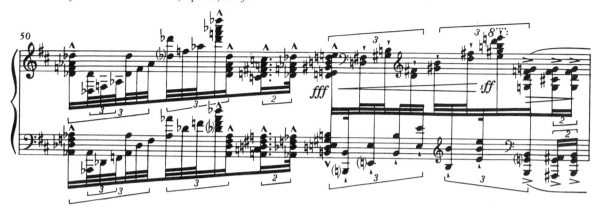

There has always been considerable criticism of the profusion of expression signs permeating Reger's scores. Walter Kolneder mentioned that even Hans Pfitzner had uttered some complaints in that regard.[9] Still, it should be noted that in the autographs these signs are set off in red ink and are therefore not as confusing to the eye as in a printed score. It would be helpful to have printed editions with colour distinctions according to Reger's own hand-written design.

♪ *Continues on following page.*

EXAMPLE 4. *Bach Variations*, op. 81, mm. 145–148

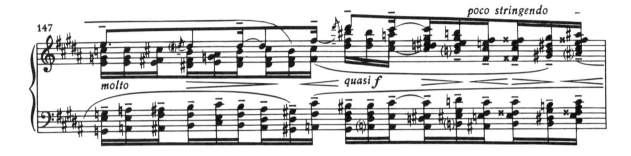

Another important element in Reger's style is the combination of a continuously growing density of texture with a commensurate increase of the dynamic level. This is usually achieved by a doubling of voices and "chordalizing" of the smallest steps, combined with a continuous amplification of the dynamics up to the nearly inevitable triple or quadruple *for-*

tissimo intended to delineate the climax, which sometimes takes the form of a hypertrophic sonic orgasm.

EXAMPLE 5.   *Bach Variations*, op. 81, mm. 381—end

It should be noted, however, that on the extreme opposite end of the scale, many pieces end in a continuous *morendo* fading out in a triple *pianissimo*.

The technique of strategically planned, carefully prepared advances towards an overwhelming final apex is especially pronounced in the magnificently constructed final fugues of his major variation works. Here we find Reger's powerful combinatory ability at its best, creating the most complex fugal structures ever found in music. Compositional "learned" devices from the baroque era, such as *stretto, inversion, diminution, augmentation*, and *retrograde*, are consistently and logically employed with a combinatory skill that has yet to be superseded. Among other conventional models providing inspiration for Max Reger, the form of the fugue as exemplified by the unsurpassed work of his beloved J.S. Bach had "captivated" him completely, challenging him to further expansions.[10] His implicit equation, "bigger equals better," however, was not always successfully resolved.

The principle of variations as such seems to be an important feature of the creative process of the composer. Reger not only has cast his most important and substantial works for solo piano in variation form (*Bach Variations*, op. 81, and *Telemann Variations*, op. 134), but his whole figurative thinking, as can be seen by the texture of many of his works, including the following excerpts, seems to be based on the continuous variation of a given musical thought.

EXAMPLE 6A.   *Humoreske*, op. 20, no. 5, mm. 1–4

EXAMPLE 6D.   *Humoreske*, op. 20, no. 5, mm. 67–70

Some have criticized the proliferation of this particular feature as manipulative and not specifically musically creative. Max Reger was even referred to as a kind of "musical engineer."[11] However, figuration as such does play an important role in Reger's musical concept and constitutes an integral part of his highly imaginative thinking. This goes hand-in-hand with his characteristic use of melodic substance as an integrated part of the overall harmonic scheme. Quite often an individualized melodic entity is not readily definable. Max Reger himself mentioned at one point that he did not write melodies in the normal sense.[12] This has attracted considerable criticism. Walter Niemann, for example, noted that in Reger's instrumental music a "personalized" melodic characteristic often cannot be found. He tried to prove this particular hypothesis by isolating the melodic substance in Reger's chamber music and came to the surprising conclusion that the melodic substance *per se* is limited to "barely understandable and seemingly senseless chains of tones."[13]

For Reger, thematic material, other than that used in his major variation works, seems to have constituted little more than a motivic inspiration, frequently displayed in short two-bar or sometimes three-bar phrases, and immediately subjected to extended modulation and sequential treatment.

EXAMPLE 7.   *Aus meinem Tagebuch*, op. 82/I, no. 4, mm. 60–63

It is very important to note that the dynamic propensities are always an integral part of the short Regerian musical phrase. Often the swell sign or beak (‹——— ———›) appears as a seemingly inevitable dynamic indicator, usually increasing to the middle and decreasing towards the end of the phrase, irrespective of the contour of the melodic design.

EXAMPLE 8.   *Zehn kleine Vortragsstücke*, op. 44, no. 1, mm. 1–4

♪ Continues on following page.

Sometimes this process is even more differentiated, as can be seen in this example.

EXAMPLE 9. *Träume am Kamin*, op. 143, no. 9, mm. 1–2

The two-bar entity frequently is used as a structural building block. Reger often ingeniously avoids the built-in danger of stereotyping multiple two-bar units by adding "interjection bars." These sometimes take the character of a reiteration of a short phrase in a different register, as is obvious in bars 17 and 22 of Example 10.

EXAMPLE 10. *Zehn kleine Vortragsstücke,* op. 44, no. 5, mm. 15–23

Reger's contrapuntal skills are proverbial. He seemed to enjoy the manipulative side of this technique and showed considerable pride in this faculty. Not only did he compose a substantial number of two- and three-voice canons as a compendium of masterly craftsmanship,[14] but he also added an obligato violin part to six sonatinas by M. Clementi, complemented the *Two-Part Inventions* by J.S. Bach with a third voice, and even infused an obligato horn part into an orchestral piece by another composer.[15]

♪ *Continues on following page.*

In studying the inherent texture of his scores, one discovers a continuous fluctuation between strict four-part writing and homophonic textures with "polyphonized" inner voice leading, obviously intended to give increased meaning and weight to the musical structure.[16]

EXAMPLE 11.   *Bach Variations*, op. 81, fugue, mm. 360–361

Unfortunately, the sometimes indiscriminate use of this type of "pseudo counterpoint," loaded with chromatic passing notes, results in a profusely thick texture, which seems to obscure rather than clearly delineate the composer's musical intentions.

A more interesting textural feature as a part of the varied figurative manipulation is the "inner voice line" or, pianistically speaking, the "inner thumb line," usually occurring in fast alternating chords. The technique of alternating hands in fast passages can be traced to Liszt, who used it extensively in various patterns of virtuosic character. However, in Max Reger's writing this stylistic element gains an additional quality, emphasizing either inner textural melodic delineations or—especially when chromaticisms are employed—creating colouristic effects, or a combination of both.

EXAMPLE 12.   *Telemann Variations*, op. 134, var. 8, mm. 1–2

EXAMPLE 13. *Sieben Charakterstücke*, op. 32, no. 2, mm. 1–2

In addition, Max Reger frequently resorts to an idiomatic articulation pattern, consisting of the grouping of two legato and two staccato notes.

EXAMPLE 14.   *Zehn kleine Klavierstücke*, op. 44, no. 2, mm. 1–4

Both these features evolved into a particularly Regerian style, most frequently encountered in his character pieces entitled *Burletta*, *Burleske*, or *Humoreske*. Here Reger has created an idiosyncratic expression which can be considered a unique contribution to the literature for the piano.

In his piano music Max Reger copied, imitated, and amalgamated many traits of other composers. Only towards the end of his life did he begin to consolidate his own style, a process which unfortunately was terminated by his untimely death.

Characteristics of other great composers, in particular Brahms, but also Schumann and Liszt, are especially apparent in Reger's earlier pieces, which have been criticized as being stylistically epigonal. But Reger very much followed his declared credo that valid artistic progress must be

"B–A–C–H ist Anfang und
Ende aller Musik."
("B–A–C–H constitutes the
beginning and end of all
music.") Handwriting by
Max Reger, 1902. (Max
Reger Institut)

based on solid historical precedents, hence his strong aversion to the
Neudeutsche Schule then in vogue and his identification with the accomplishments of the musical past, especially with those of J.S. Bach, whom he
considered "the beginning and end of all music."[17]

He obviously wanted to learn from his predecessors just as a painter
might copy the works of old masters in order to become familiar with their
techniques. This may explain his strong identification with the compositional techniques of Brahms, who with Bach influenced Reger the most.
The composer himself mentioned the similarity of his piano style to
Brahmsian traits like the rhythmical idiosyncrasy two against three, the
doubling of the third, and the treatment of the left hand.[18] This is clearly
evident, for instance, in the passionate *Rhapsody* (dedicated to the "spirit"
of Brahms) from the *Six Morceaux pour le Piano*, op. 24, with its abundance of stylistic elements borrowed from his admired predecessor.

EXAMPLE 15.   *Six Morceaux pour le Piano*, op. 24, mm. 1–4

In *Resignation*, the fifth piece of the *Sieben Fantasiestücke*, op. 26, dated the day of Brahms's death, Reger characteristically quotes the main theme of the slow movement of the *Fourth Symphony* by Brahms.

EXAMPLE 16.   *Sieben Fantasiestücke*, op. 26, no. 5, mm. 51–56

Further examples of the influence of the texture of Brahms's music on Reger's style are seen in the chordal structure and the widely-spaced accompaniment figures of another of the *Fantasiestücke*, op. 26.

EXAMPLE 17.   *Sieben Fantasiestücke*, op. 26, no. 6, mm. 94–97

As curiosities, Reger's two metamorphoses of Chopin's *Berceuse*, op. 57, should be mentioned here. They are revealing attempts of a total stylistic imitation and perfect examples of a particular compositional procedure which Zofia Lissa called "an interpretation, in which one work *ante factum* becomes a source of inspiration and a model for a new work."[19]

EXAMPLE 18.   Chopin, *Berceuse*, op. 57, mm. 1–4

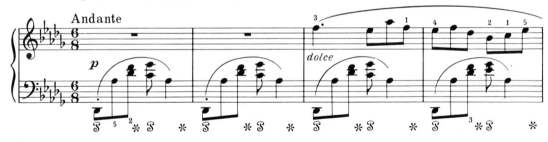

EXAMPLE 19. *Aus meinem Tagebuch*, op. 82/II, no. 9, mm. 1–3

EXAMPLE 20. *Träume am Kamin*, op. 143, no. 12, mm. 1–3

Sudden changes of register and surprising dynamic contrasts, often combined as a double effect, could also be considered a special recurring stylistic trait in Reger's compositions. These features are employed with great skill to enliven the musical structure and to add textural and dynamic variety. Quite often they are a reflection of the boisterous humour Reger displayed in real life as well as in so much of his music.

♪ *Continues on following page.*

EXAMPLE 21.   *Sieben Fantasiestücke*, op. 26, no. 7, mm. 54–58

These are but a few of the more obvious and important features characteristic of Reger's work. Others, less obvious but still important, will
quickly become evident in the course of a more detailed exploration of
Reger's most important works for the piano, to which we now turn.

4

A VACILLATING OEUVRE

Within the controversy surrounding Max Reger as a composer we also find polarized opinions about the underlying motives for his extraordinary creativity. A sympathetic view would stress the sincere, nearly missionary effort of a composer deeply concerned about the direction music was taking in his time, trying to counteract this trend by a conscious proliferation of his own creative work. The unsympathetic mind might instead conclude that the composer was driven by an indiscriminate creativity, endlessly churning out work after work and finding satisfaction only in robot-like productivity. A somewhat more probing insight is provided by Rainer Cadenbach, according to whom, "one can be sure that Max Reger compensated for his personal problems by work, accomplishment and production."[1]

As always, the truth is found somewhere in the middle. Certainly, considering the comparatively short life span of the composer, the sheer volume of Reger's output is overwhelming. Furthermore, having always had a phalanx of eager publishers at hand, Max Reger anxiously strove to have every composition published and possibly performed as soon as it was finished. He seemed to derive some personal gratification from the fact that he was able to work effectively under the continuous pressure of deadlines for publication and performance. Although he was constantly complaining about the overwhelming stress in his hectic life, he also expressed satisfaction in his efforts to transfer the baroque tradition of compositional craftsmanship, which he admired so much in J.S. Bach, into the romantic era. That included the ability to compose on request and under the pressure of deadlines.

While Brahms, in a kind of final house-cleaning, was critical enough to destroy an unknown number of compositions he considered unworthy of publication, no such action is reported of Reger. This does not imply that Reger was uncritical. He wrote his publisher that he was providing only the best and emphatically denounced quite a number of early works, calling them "terrible sins of youth" and trying to prevent their publication.[2] He also told musicians in strong terms which pieces he considered "totally old-fashioned" and not worth any public performance.[3] Still, the fact remains that Reger's work—especially in the field of piano music—shows considerable fluctuations of compositional quality, ranging from the most simplistic banality to profound inspirational sublimity.

Thus the intent of this study as an introduction to the solo piano music of Max Reger is *not* to discuss all piano works in detail. On the contrary, by focusing on the most characteristic compositions, it aims to provide a reasonably encompassing extract of and introduction to the maze of compositions by Max Reger available for solo piano. Such a procedure requires highly individual value judgements based on personal understanding and preference. Of course, such subjectivity is not intended to be taken as sagacity *ex cathedra*. However, limiting the focus thus on what can conceivably be considered artistically the most important, valuable, and representative works should provide a solid basis of understanding for the reader, who can then make further explorations, if so inclined.

Among the 146 numbered compositions we find 21 works for solo piano, some containing up to 35 single pieces (such as in the four-volume *Aus meinem Tagebuch*, op. 82). For the purpose of this discussion it seems practical to allot these piano works somewhat chronologically to three periods—early, middle, and late—that could be seen as vaguely delineating various stylistic stages of Reger's development in his writing for piano. The early period, roughly corresponding to what is generally known as the "Weiden Period," will include all works written in Wiesbaden and Weiden

A letter to Henriette Schelle, dated November 26, 1901. (Max Reger Institut)

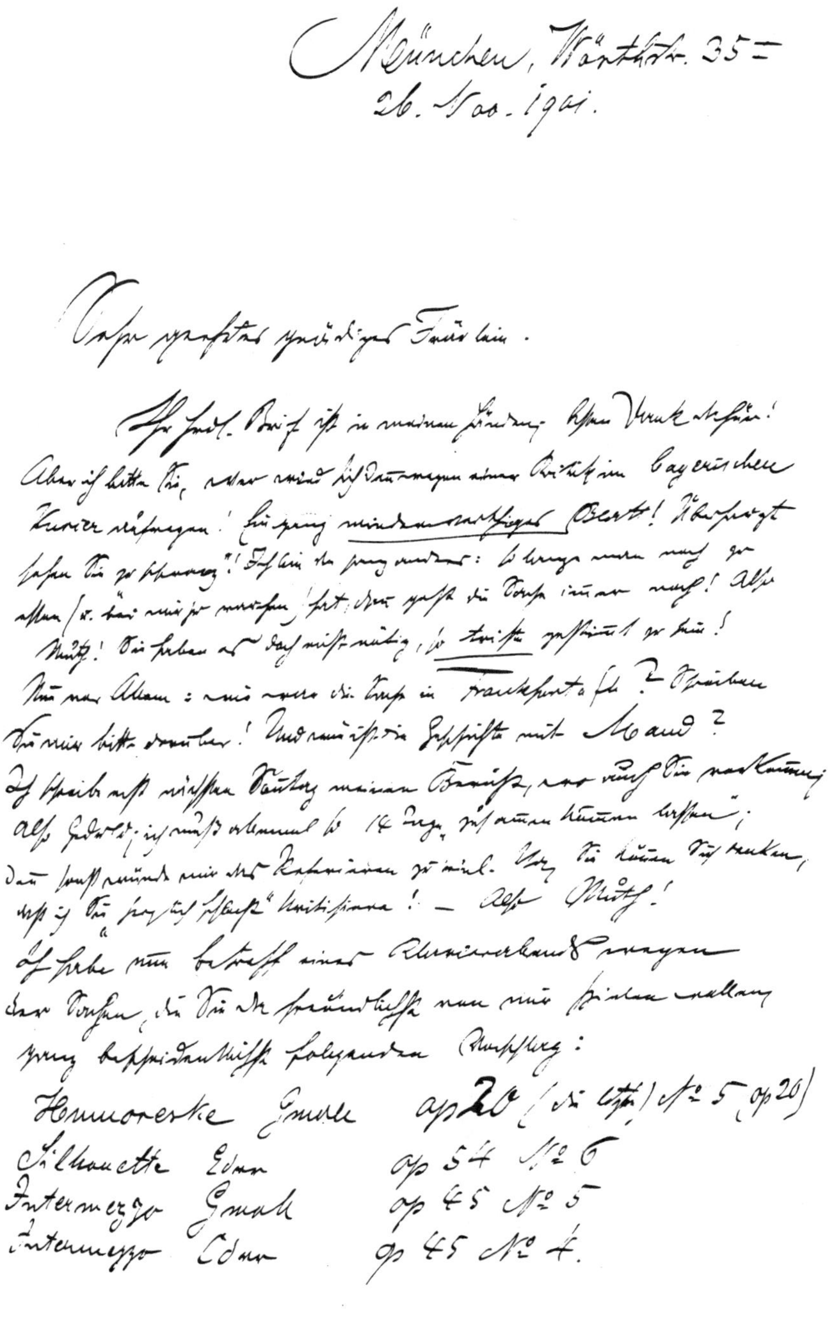
München, Wörthstr. 35
26. Nov. 1901.

Sehr geehrtes gnädiges Fräulein.

Humoreske Gmoll op 20 (die letzte) No 5 (op 20)
Silhouette Edur op 54 No 6
Intermezzo Gmoll op 45 No 5
Intermezzo Cdur op 45 No 4.

die Resignation des Meininger Herzog — bitte ich
Sie dringendst, nicht mehr zu spielen; doch
möchte ich für mich natürlich davorlesen.

Aber mit den haben (nachsehend seits) aus gegebenen
Würden wünsche die Herr, wo nun die Reg esche
thenen, umsomehr sich doch ihnen so sehr zu wünscht ist,
(namentlich die Besitz, und dass die Probschrift) ein
Meininger nachdrück eingewinnen. Also bitte bitte sehr!

Nun, wo ich jetzt wenigstens keine Spuren mehr
Reger zu spielen; aber ich bin's so sehr gewöhnt,
nicht ausgenützt zu werden!

Oder ist's mit Clarinettensonate in Meiningen?

Aber was haben Sie da neue (nachgeschrieben
geschrieben? Das soll nach Innuia hin!

Frei lanzierens so ganz fertig, und Sie
fürfallen ich in Kurz, wovon hernach eine
fleißigst mitzugeben hätten miteinander.

Noch eine Bitte: Lieben Sie das Sichmachen!

Leben Sie die nächste Gelegenheit meine Sachen
möglichst ... zu ... . Z. B. Op 44
36 20 ... Op ... Ihnen ... haben auch
Op 22; ich lege Ihnen ein Verzeichniß bei.
Bitte, thun Sie das; ich werde Ihnen früher
... Die Verzeichnisse liegen
in dem Intermezzi, Op 45, welche auch dieser
... zur ... Freude an Sie abgehen!

Bitte, ... Sie meine ... Schrift;
allein ich habe eben zu ... u. ... schreibe
auch, wo ... anbringen. Also
freundliche Entschuldigung über die Schrift.

Nur sehen Sie bitte mal zu, daß ... aus dem
Clavierauszug in ... ... wird,
daß Manch der Seite aber einen ...

Flügel zur Benützung haben? Oder ich frage zurück, werden Sie Dehn, der gestern mit größter Gründlich-
keit üben? ...

Mit den besten u. herzlichsten Grüßen u. auf
Wiedersehen im Januar.
Ihr
sehr ergebenster, reichster
Max Reger

(up to 1900), with the exception of opp. 44, 45, and 53, works that already show increasingly new characteristic features justifying their inclusion in the middle period. Works discussed under that heading, usually referred to as Reger's "Wild Munich Period" (up to 1907), here also encompass for practical reasons all the pieces of opp. 82 and 89, although some of these are of a later date. The late period culminating in the so-called "Free Jena Style" covers the rest of the piano works that have opus numbers (up to 1916). A final section deals with a number of compositions without opus numbers created throughout all three periods. Such a division of a continuously evolving oeuvre is by its very definition arbitrary and is employed here only for convenience. In view of the fact that the borderlines between such exactly delineated work periods are by no means clear, the question certainly might be asked whether it makes any sense at all to subject Reger's complete oeuvre to a strict division into a beginning, a middle, and an end period. However, two pinnacles in Reger's work point to a certain logic in the chosen groupings.

As a significant climax in Reger's organ oeuvre, the *Fantasie und Fuge über B–A–C–H*, op. 46, composed in 1900, represents a suitable compositional marker between a first and second period. The same may be said about the *Variationen und Fuge über ein Thema von J.A. Hiller*, op. 100, composed in 1907, as a marker between the second and third periods. This work can be considered a significant milestone in Reger's increasing use of the orchestra as an expanded medium of expression and points directly to his major achievement in variation form, the *Variationen und Fuge über ein Thema von W.A. Mozart*, op. 132, composed two years before his untimely death.

The majority of Reger's oeuvre for piano consists of relatively short romantic character pieces modelled along the basic A–B–A scheme rampant around the turn of the century, ranging from the more shallow prototypes by Theodor Kirchner and Adolf Jensen to artistic masterpieces like some of the *Intermezzi* by Brahms. On the other side of the spectrum tower the two gigantic variation works, the *Bach Variations*, op. 81, and the *Telemann Variations*, op. 134. In between we find *Vier Sonatinen*, op. 89; *Sechs Präludien und Fugen*, op. 99; *Fünf Spezialstudien nach Chopin*; the *111 Kanons durch alle Dur- und Molltonarten*; and various single genre pieces. Aside from the shorter, more transparent sonatinas, Reger never

used the sonata form for a major work for solo piano, although he continuously cultivated it in his extensive chamber music. The lack of a major
sonata for solo piano should come as no surprise, given the sociological
and commercial situation at that time, which was generally more conducive to the prolific production of smaller character pieces. There was,
after all, a great demand for this kind of music from amateur musicians. In
a sense this type of demand has shifted today to more passive approaches
to music that keep recording companies alive.

In order to allow for the utmost conciseness and clarity, discussion of
the most important works will proceed within a chronological framework
represented by opus numbers. In quite a few collections of character pieces
only a few might warrant detailed attention, and the rest will be mentioned
more or less in passing. The aim of this procedure is to concentrate on
works that are representative of Max Reger's best achievements in the field
of piano music. This focused approach should provide the general reader
as well as the pianist with a concentrated sampling that has some practical
use, rather than with an encyclopedic survey beneficial only to the musicol-
ogist. In this context attention should be drawn to William Thomas Hopkins's comprehensive, detailed study of Reger's shorter piano pieces.[4]

WORKS WITH OPUS NUMBERS

EARLY PERIOD

Although Reger denounced quite a number of his early works for solo
piano up to op. 20 and including op. 25,[5] some of these pieces may be
worth mentioning, especially if one takes a certain pedagogical value into
consideration; however, the *Sieben Walzer*, op. 11 (1893), and the *Lose
Blätter*, op. 13, composed in 1894 for Riemann's child, are of little artistic
value. Reger himself admitted in a letter to Adalbert Lindner that the
Walzer, op. 11, "should be considered only a gift to Augener with no artistic interest on my part."[6] The fourteen pieces of op. 13, although in some
ways more concise, provide examples of indiscriminate stylistic plagiarisms
from composers like Schubert (op. 13, no. 9), Schumann (op. 13, no. 4),
Chopin (op. 13, no. 13), Mendelssohn (op. 13, no. 10), Liszt (op. 13, no.
13), and Brahms (op. 13, no. 14). In their compositional intent one could

consider op. 11 and op. 13 basically a *sequitur* to the op. 9 and op. 10 duets composed in response to a request by the publisher Augener, who wanted pieces that would sell and not collect mildew on the shelf like some of the earlier chamber music works that were obviously not commercial successes. With op. 17, however, the work becomes more interesting.

Aus der Jugendzeit, op. 17 (1895)

These twenty piano pieces with imaginative titles were originally published in three volumes in 1902 (vol. I, nos. 1–7; vol. II, nos. 8–14; vol. III, nos. 15–20). A selection of fourteen pieces was also published in 1931.[7] The work seems to have been born out of Max Reger's activity as a piano teacher at the Fuchs'sche Konservatorium in Wiesbaden and is definitely aimed at the young piano student.

Unlike more balanced collections of piano pieces "for the young," such as those by Robert Schumann or Walter Niemann, this set is a mixture of some quite imaginative and pedagogically valuable pieces on the one hand and some rather trifling miniatures on the other, which devalue the set as a whole. Two pieces, no. 5 and no. 6, warrant attention from the pedagogical point of view.

♪ *Continues on following page.*

Op. 17, no. 5, *Über Stock und Stein*

Here we have an useful study for wrist and finger staccato in fast tempo based on a healthy musical substance, which is convincing and enjoyable at the same time. Flexible and contrasting dynamics permeate the piece. Both hands are equally employed, which is certainly an advantage compared to the usual style of the genre piece at that time. This seems to be a good piece for a student recital. In the Breitkopf & Härtel *Gesamtausgabe* a discrepancy in the notation occurs: in b. 11 the last eighth note is notated as a G sharp, in the parallel passage in b. 39 as an A. Both versions are valid solutions.

EXAMPLE 22A.   Op. 17, no. 5, m. 11

EXAMPLE 22B.   Op. 17, no. 5, m. 39

Op. 17, no. 6, *Was die Großmutter erzählt*

In some ways this short composition consisting of a number of loosely but subtly interconnected contrasting sections represents a microcosm of Max Reger's imagination. It shows in a simple way the continuous process of variation and evolution of both musical ideas and compositional elements that is so characteristic of this composer. The following examples show various textural metamorphoses of a single motif and its manifold combinations.

EXAMPLE 23A.   Op. 17, no. 6, mm. 1–12

EXAMPLE 23B.   Op. 17, no. 6, mm. 37–44

EXAMPLE 23C.   Op. 17, no. 6, mm. 54–60

A number of musical and technical challenges give a teacher ample opportunities to draw the young student's attention not only to subtle articulation, meticulous phrasing, and varied, often strongly contrasting, dynamics, but also to skilful voice leading which is important in the sections in four-part writing. Mm. 34–35 present some problems with respect to rhythmical coordination. In comparison to the parallel passage, the differentiation in the bass line, mm. 19–21, is rather subtle, but very effective. This piece is suitable for pedagogical purposes.

Improvisationen, op. 18 (1897)

In this collection Max Reger suddenly focuses on the piano as a solo instrument and explores its sonorities in a way similar to the treatment this instrument received in his early chamber music works. In spite of many stylistic features clearly traceable to Brahms and Liszt, a number of compositional traits point to the emergence of an identifiable Regerian style. The most obvious characteristic is the abundance of polyphonic writing within veiled harmonic progressions. The contrasting chordal textures vary. Some are quite pianistic in their virtuosic patterns; others, with their continuous suspensions in all voices, allude to the organ as a more adequate medium. Such chordal structures (similar to those in Example 39) are difficult to realize on the piano, since the necessary polyphonic transparency should be maintained. An immaculate finger legato combined with subtle use of the pedal is probably the answer here, while in other cases the virtuosic chordal patterns require a mature technical prowess. Note, for instance, the Schumannesque texture of the following example.

EXAMPLE 24.　Op. 18, no. 5, mm. 90–94

These pieces (except for no. 7) display some imaginative concepts and interesting compositional elements. They are also a clear manifestation of the personal problems and difficulties Max Reger encountered during the time of composition. They could hold their own on the concert stage, and fall well within the tradition of the fully developed character piece of the romantic era.

The first edition of the *Improvisationen*, published by Augener & Co. in London in 1902, contained an additional piece (no. 8 in C minor) which was omitted in the subsequent Schott edition of 1910 and later published as *Etude Brillante* in a single edition without an opus number.

The most rewarding pieces seem to be nos. 4, 5, and 6. As a stylistic contrast each or all three as a group could be successfully incorporated in any concert program.

Op. 18, no. 4 (*Andante semplice*)

The *semplice* A–B–A structure is permeated by the wide-spaced texture so characteristic of Brahms (compare, for example, the *Intermezzo*, op. 118, no. 2, or the *Ballades*, op. 10). The middle section in particular shows all the important features of this style of writing: expanded tonal range, widely spaced chords, and thickened texture, resulting in opulent romantic sonorities. Rhythmical features like two against three (note mm. 22–26) further intensify the Brahmsian flavour. Although not specifically indicated, the use of ample pedal is certainly an important part of the interpretation if the compact sound spectrum envisaged by the composer is to be realized efficiently.

EXAMPLE 25.   Op. 18, no. 4, mm. 18–26

Op. 18, no. 5 (*Moderato, ma marcato*)

The massive beginning with its strong *ff* dynamics and full chords in dotted rhythms radiates the feeling of a titanic struggle, for which even the more soothing passages that follow provide no relief. Again the sonorities point to Brahms and the texture to Liszt. Mm. 56–57 contain a direct quote of the first theme of the first movement of Brahms's *Fourth Symphony*. Technically quite challenging and full of true pathos, this impressive rhapsodic work is worth studying and could serve as a particularly successful complement in any concert program.

EXAMPLE 26.   Op. 18, no. 5, mm. 53–58

Op. 18, no. 6 (*Allegretto con grazia*)

In strong contrast to op. 18, no. 5, Max Reger here emphasizes the *grazioso* character, again with strong reminiscences of Brahms, whose music had at that time an immense influence on Reger, who called him "the great Valhalla."[8] The contrasting middle section set in an A–B–A form shows Reger's general tendency to emphasize imitative entries by *marcato* indications. So prevalent in the extended fugues of his large variation works, this particular feature occurs here within the context of a canon, as if Reger wanted to make sure that his art of counterpoint was not overlooked.

EXAMPLE 27.   Op. 18, no. 6, mm. 27–30

However, all this is done with much taste and sophistication, and the result is an imaginative and enjoyable piece.

Fünf Humoresken, op. 20 (1898)

In these popular pieces, the first of this type written during the so-called "Weiden Period," Max Reger for the first time displays some of his own idiosyncratic stylistic traits in the genre of the character piece. The inherent *capriccioso*, *humoresque*, or *burlesque* character above all seems to be an amicable reflection of Reger's humorous personality and his intrinsic affinity to the jocular as such. It is remarkable how intelligently Reger deployed the compositional equivalents and fused them into a characteristic language of his own.

All pieces show an abundance of sophisticated articulation with a preference for the staccato. In particular, the characteristic alternation of two slurred and two staccato sixteenth notes occurs frequently.

EXAMPLE 28.   Op. 20, no. 2, mm. 37–39

This figurative pattern must be considered a compositional trademark of Max Reger, used over and over again, finding its apotheosis in the towering fugue of the *Bach Variations*. It was already recognized as such during his lifetime.[9] The same can be said about the pianistic patterns of alternation between the two hands, often resulting in melodic patterns within a chordal context.

EXAMPLE 29.   Op. 20, no. 4, mm. 80–85

This is, of course, an expansion of a well-known Lisztian technique. However, the emphasis seems to be on melodic intensification evoking at the same time brilliant virtuosic sound spectra. Other features of the burlesque style include strong dynamic contrasts, sudden changes of register, a preference for the higher registers, and sudden changes of tempo.

All five pieces are structured according to the conventional A–B–A' pattern, with A' being a figurative elaboration or intensification of A. Three of the *Fünf Humoresken* end in *ppp*—another indicator of Max Reger's highly sensitive humorous style.

With exception of op. 20, no. 2, the character of which is more that of a rhapsodic burlesque incorporating nonmusical connotations,[10] all pieces live up to the expectation evoked by the term *Humoreske*. Although of moderate technical difficulty, they are pianistically very rewarding compositions and suitable for teaching and inclusion in concert programs. They could even be programmed as a set, although a selection of three might be more advisable. The most balanced choice seems to be nos. 1, 3, and 5.

Op. 20, no. 1 (*Allegretto grazioso*)
In this concise work (perhaps the most often performed of the five) melodic
and figurative elements are well balanced. The continuously changing two-
bar patterns are particularly obvious here.

EXAMPLE 30A.   Op. 20, no. 1, mm. 8–15

In contrast to the vivid character of the A section, the chordal middle
part in F sharp minor with its more sustained pace and its setting in the
lower register of the piano evokes a darker mood, while the harmonies are
reminiscent of Edvard Grieg.

EXAMPLE 30B.   Op. 20, no. 1, mm. 16–21

AUGUSTANA UNIVERSITY COLLEGE
LIBRARY

The exquisitely detailed articulation and a multitude of dynamic indications found in this piece require of the performer much attention and technical skill. Although the composer himself did not think particularly highly of this *Humoreske*, it is certainly one of the best teaching pieces for the intermediate level student.

Op. 20, no. 3 (*Andante grazioso*)

In addition to the *Andante grazioso* marking, Reger emphasizes the desired character with the annotation *leggiero e sempre grazioso*. A relatively transparent texture and quite diversified rhythmical structure within a limited ambitus enhances the horizontal motion of the melodic flow. The Schumannesque middle section contains some motifs juxtaposed bar by bar, which—typically for Reger—are immediately varied (see Example 31). However, the strong contrasts usually so common in a Regerian *Humoreske* are lacking.

EXAMPLE 31.   Op. 20, no. 3, mm. 38–41

The piece is constructed from short musical ideas and similar figurative elements mainly contained in two-bar phrases. Dynamic changes are frequent and hardly any phrase, even as short as a bar, is found without the stereotypic dynamic beaks indicative of a swell towards the middle of the figure and back (see also Example 8).

Op. 20, no. 5 (*Vivace assai*)

Reger loved this piece, performed it himself quite a number of times, and recorded it on the Welte-Mignon System. His playing displays a featherlike brilliancy, as glittering cascades seem to evoke intoxicating fragrances wafting through the air. The rhythmical strictness so typical of modern interpretations is replaced by a charming freedom and horizontal flexibility of a degree one can hardly imagine being possible. This recording[11] documents Reger's interpretative magic, frequently referred to by his contemporaries.

As a composition this is probably the most equilibristic of all the humoresques by Reger. The prevalence of the high register combined with *una corda*, *pp*, and *staccatissimo* to be realized in a very fast tempo creates a glittering sound spectrum sometimes reminiscent of Liszt.

EXAMPLE 32.   Op. 20, no. 5, mm. 18–22

Virtuosic figurations common in romantic piano technique dominate this scintillating creation. They are juxtaposed with strongly contrasting *ff* interjections with hemiolic connotations, sometimes even eliminating the rhythmic parameter of the 6/8 time signature. The same is true of the middle section, in which the rhythmical definition is several times suspended and underlined harmonically by weak phrase endings (see Example 33).

EXAMPLE 33.   Op. 20, no. 5, mm. 34–50

The *tenuto* signs on nearly every chord could be emphasized through a "velvet touch," with the hand "sinking" into the keyboard, although a continuous flow must be maintained, especially when the pulsation transcends the meter (note mm. 37–38, mm. 44–45, or mm. 49–50). All in all, this piece represents a climax in Max Reger's early writing and should be performed more often.

Six Morceaux pour le Piano, op. 24 (1898)

The choice of the French language for the titles in the first edition by Augener & Co., London, seems to indicate that these compositions were intended to serve a publisher's need to offer another group of commercially viable salon-type pieces to an obviously insatiable market for that kind of musical product. The shallowness of this contribution to the commercial gamut is deplorable and, with respect to compositional value, rather embarrassing. As in the earlier collections of op. 11, op. 13, and op. 18, several superficial compositions are lumped together with one or two pieces of better quality. Even the assumption that Max Reger might have considered these collections as a kind of testing ground for the exploration of various modes and styles of composition does not justify their publication.

The titles of the six pieces are *Valse-Impromptu* (no. 1), *Menuet* (no. 2), *Rêverie fantastique* (no. 3), *Un moment musical* (no. 4), *Chant de la nuit* (no. 5), and *Rhapsodie* (no. 6). The only piece worth mentioning here might be the *Rhapsodie*, an extended work of considerable impact.

♪ *Continues on following page.*

Op. 24, no. 6, *Rhapsodie*

The dedication *"Den Manen J. Brahms'"* certainly is indicative of Reger's intention to compose a piece that reflected not only the style of Brahms's writing, but also the somber mood which so often permeates his music. These characteristics are adequately reflected in this piece, the longest and most substantial of the whole collection.

EXAMPLE 34.   Op. 24, no. 6, mm. 23–28

Reger, of course, must have been quite aware of the superb formal proportions in Brahms's music. It therefore does not come as any surprise that he conceived a rather symmetrical form (A–B)–C–(A'–B'), with open as well as hidden motivic interrelationships playing important roles. These unifying aspects counteract in a positive way the characteristic Regerian meandering through a rather short-phrased melodic landscape. Although in many instances deceptively Brahmsian, the diction is quite different and somewhat erratic.

EXAMPLE 35. Op. 24, no. 6, mm. 12–14

Nevertheless, this piece has many intrinsic qualities, most notably in respect to the treatment of harmony, that point to the mature Reger. The performer requires a tremendous amount of imagination to link together the loose chain of contrasting moods within a boldly shifting harmonic network. As a document revealing the irresistible emotional compulsion of the young Max Reger, this composition presents itself as a rewarding object for study, if not performance.

Aquarelle, Kleine Tonbilder, op. 25 (1897/98)

Neither particularly important nor in any way exemplary of Reger's style, this collection of shorter genre pieces shows low to average compositional quality. Niels Gade had already used the title *Aquarell* for a tone-painting of lighter and transparent character written in a Schumannesque style. However, in this collection there seems to be no discernible association between the title and individual pieces—*Canzonetta* (no. 1), *Humoreske* (no. 2), *Impromptu* (no. 3), *Nordische Ballade* (no. 4), and *Mazurka* (no. 5)—in which many heterogeneous conventional stylistic elements are combined rather indiscriminately.

Some compositional coherence, however, is found in the evocative fourth piece, which was originally part of the *Grüße an die Jugend* but was replaced there by a curious piece jointly composed by Reger and Adalbert Lindner. Since Reger dedicated this collection to Edvard Grieg, it is not surprising that the *Nordische Ballade* has a strong folkloric flavour reminiscent of the Norwegian master.

Op. 25, no. 4, *Nordische Ballade*

In the beginning of the piece Reger departs from his usual melodic concept of short two-bar phrases and establishes a longer melodic line within a rather reduced texture. The focused unison voice leading in a low register creates a somber mood. That Reger had a sixth sense for the employment of varied textural elements as a strong means of expression is quite obvious in this piece, as it evolves within a loosely knit formal context in subtle metamorphoses of the original melodic substance. Indications of articulation and dynamics are as varied as ever, including *tenuto* signs above notes emphasizing melodic connotations and even a quadruple *pianissimo*.

EXAMPLE 36.   Op. 25, no. 4, mm. 45–47

Some passages require considerable technical control and differentiation of touch within one hand.

EXAMPLE 37.   Op. 25, no. 4, mm. 48–50

The intermediate piano student intending to expand skills in the area of balancing sonorities with the proper use of the pedals might find some suitable training in this composition.

Sieben Fantasiestücke, op. 26 (1898)

The pieces in this collection generally show more originality and compositional substance than anything previous, with the exception of the *Humoresken,* op. 20. They all have titles: *Elegy* (no. 1), *Scherzo* (no. 2), *Barcarole* (no. 3), *Humoreske* (no. 4), *Resignation* (no. 5), *Impromptu* (no. 6), and *Capriccio* (no. 7). They show a consolidation of the growing process towards a more genuine personal language within the composer's solo piano writing. Clearly discernible now are:

1. Figurative exchanges in both hands in fast speed, usually in staccato, resulting in the creation of an inner chromatic line as a background figuration sharpening the awareness of the harmonic progressions.

EXAMPLE 38.   Op. 26, no. 7, mm. 11–15

2. Intricate polyphonic textures filled abundantly with suspensions and syncopations that tend to obscure clear harmonic delineations.

EXAMPLE 39. Op. 26, no. 5, mm. 10–15

♪ Continues on following page.

3. Parallel moving lines, usually in sixteenth note values supported by harmonic notes on eighth note values, resulting in an increasingly dense texture.

EXAMPLE 40.   Op. 26, no. 2, mm. 4–5

4. Frequent appearance of the well-known Regerian "articulation grouping" of two slurred sixteenth notes followed by two staccato sixteenth notes.

EXAMPLE 41.   Op. 26, no. 4, mm. 13–15

In op. 26, essential characteristics of Reger's later, more mature piano style are in the process of emerging from dominating traits established by his romantic predecessors, mainly Brahms. Thus it seems nearly inevitable that special reference is made to that particular composer, whose date of death Reger added to the title of the fifth piece, *Resignation*. The most convincing compositions of this collection are no. 5 and no. 6; they could very well be included in a concert program.

Op. 26, no. 5, *Resignation* ("3 April 1897—J. Brahms[†]")

Representing a deeply felt homage to Brahms on his death, this piece evokes sadness and mourning. Brahms's compositional procedures are obvious everywhere, in the melodic and harmonic substance as well as in the texture and figuration, dynamics, colour, and sonorities. Here Reger expresses deep reverence for a model which influenced so many of his compositions for solo piano. Entirely appropriate in this context, he even quotes at the end a theme from the second movement of Brahms's *Fourth Symphony*. This concentrated and formally balanced composition is quite suitable for concert performance. However, it might be helpful to make the audience aware in some way of the circumstances of its creation (see Example 16).

♪ *Continues on following page.*

A short example taken from an *Intermezzo* by Brahms shows similar stylistic and textural elements.

EXAMPLE 42. Brahms, op. 118, no. 2, mm. 107–116

Op. 26, no. 6, *Impromptu*

This extended *agitato* in A–B–A' form again reflects the spirit of Brahms. Virtuosic writing and extreme contrasts in dynamics and texture prevail. The calmer middle section based on a three-note motif is substantial enough to hold the two main sections together. The composer accumulates massive chordal sound blocks towards towering climax points, dynamically reaching *ffff* in m. 160.

EXAMPLE 43. Op. 26, no. 6, mm. 158–161

Whether such extreme dynamic indications require the commensurate decibel levels that are possible on modern concert grands or whether they should be interpreted more as controlled, expansive sound patterns is a question of individual taste. It should not be forgotten, however, that the usual concomitant parallel increase in textural density in itself should render the meaning of those dynamic markings relative rather than absolute.

The contrasting dynamics are especially striking when, for example, a progression is presented first in *ff* (mm. 47 ff.) and then varied in *ppp* (mm. 170 ff.). Frequently the similarity of the texture to that of Max Reger's organ style contributes to a magical effect in this stormy piece, which ends, typically for the composer, in a soothing triple *pianissimo*. It is worthwhile to perform such a substantial work, even if it does not yet reflect the consolidated compositional language of his later pieces. It is, however, indicative of the 26-year-old Reger's ambitious yearning to be seen as equal to the great masters. Reger once implored his faithful interpreter, Henriette Schelle, not to play this piece any more.[12] Ms. Schelle wisely disregarded his wishes and performed the piece in Berlin on March 21, 1905.

Sieben Charakterstücke, op. 32 (1899)

Entitled *Improvisation* (no. 1), *Capriccio (Eine Studie)* (no. 2), *Burleske* (no. 3), *Intermezzo* (no. 4), *Intermezzo* (no. 5), *Humoreske* (no. 6), and *Impromptu* (no. 7), these compositions are mainly of a passionately virtuosic character. The compositional quality varies from piece to piece. The most individualized can be seen as mirroring the inner turmoil the composer experienced at that time. They are also the most impressive and best suited for public performance. Two more technically oriented compositions could be used profitably as studies to deal with specific problems: the *Capriccio* (no. 2), for fast alternation of hands creating the typical "inner chromaticisms" and brilliant note repetitions, and the *Burleske* (no. 3), for dynamically contrasting, powerful staccato passages that require tremendous stamina in the fast tempo indicated.

EXAMPLE 44.   Op. 32, no. 2, mm. 49–54

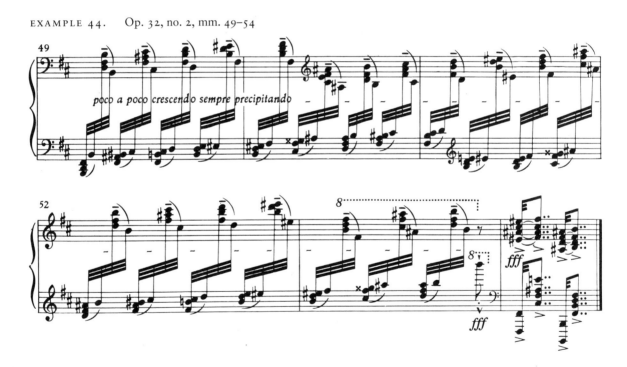

EXAMPLE 45. Op. 32, no. 3, mm. 31–35

The only weak composition in this set appears to be the *Intermezzo* (no. 5). The *Humoreske* (no. 6) and two of the three passionate pieces, the *Intermezzo* (no. 4) and the *Impromptu* (no. 7), are truly impressive concert pieces comparable to similar works by the early Skryabin. It is deplorable that they are hardly ever performed in public.

Op. 32, no. 4, *Intermezzo*

This highly virtuosic *Nachtstück* in F sharp minor seems to reflect inner and outer struggles Max Reger experienced during the period of his life in which it was written. In seeking acceptance by the then important musical circles he suffered considerably from real or imagined rejection. Seldom has a composer revealed his state of mind more apparently than Reger did in this work. He follows closely the stylistic models of the dramatic romantic character piece, including agitated broken chord patterns, strongly fluctuating dynamics, and expanded sonorities, which require the ample use of the pedal. Gerhard Wünsch has called this piece "a highly successful synthesis of Lisztian pianistic figuration and Brahmsian spirit in a yet very personal attitude."[13] With the exception of certain unusual harmonic progressions (see mm. 14–15), the use of chromatic notes for colouring purposes (m. 12), and some canonic treatment (mm. 41–42), Reger stays within the established compositional techniques of the romantic era.

EXAMPLE 46.   Op. 32, no. 4, mm. 1–6

Op. 32, no. 6, *Humoreske*

The indicated *prestissimo assai* shows that the composer expects the utmost in equilibristic piano technique to execute the typical Regerian features related to texture and articulation. A pertinent example of Reger's complex formal structure, the A section contains two different musical ideas, the second of which consists of imitative entries (see mm. 14 ff.) that very quickly grow into a dense articulate chordal texture with a maximum of dynamic contrast.

EXAMPLE 47.   Op. 32, no. 6, mm. 23–26

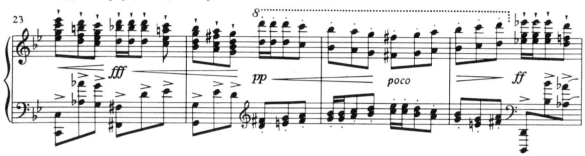

The more meditative, rather short B section is a fine example of Max Reger's irregular phrase structure, so characteristic of his "musical prose." The chromaticisms in this part strongly contribute to its evocative character. A considerably shortened and altered A' section with pianistic patterns reminiscent of Liszt (note the cascades in mm. 85–89) concludes this effective piece. The ascending figuration at the end reaches B flat""—a pitch which was not yet available on pianos in the composer's time. In order to perform successfully this brilliant concert piece in Reger's well-established humoresque style, the performer must have a highly sophisticated agility literally at his or her fingertips, without which the required virtuosic lightness cannot be achieved.

Op. 32, no. 7, *Impromptu*

Quite a number of stylistic elements usually found in Skryabin or Rakhmaninov are characteristic features and important compositional traits in this passionate piece, including, for instance, broken chords in quintuplets (as in mm. 1–3), extreme dynamic contrasts (*ppp* versus *fff*, as in mm. 56–57), and three against four in fast tempo (as in mm. 10 ff.). The loosely structured, multi-sectional piece evolves from a three-note motif and its inversion, found mainly in the dominating section.

EXAMPLE 48A.   Op. 32, no. 7, mm. 1–2

EXAMPLE 48B.   Op. 32, no. 7, mm. 6–8

The growth of the inverted motif to four and five notes and the subsequent shift of the figuration within the 6/4 meter reveals Reger's "evolutionary" method of composition.

Powerful virtuosic outbursts occur four times, interrupted by short meditative interjections, the character of which also determines the *ppp adagio* ending. It seems important not to overlook the chromatically descending inner voice in the final *meno mosso*, emphasized by *tenuto* markings (dashes on every note). In a performance it might be advisable to use larger arm motions for every note and descend into the keys with a flexible wrist in order to create a cushioned sound desirable for the required expression.

The performer should be aware how the striking dualism of the contrasting elements, best characterized by "strong" (active, aggressive) versus "weak" (intimate, meditative), is dissolved by Reger in the end. It is certainly of symbolic significance that the composer transforms the "weak" into the "strong" by giving the final say to the musical material which is the nondominating force throughout the piece, although its shape is obviously derived from the inversion of the initial melodic motif.

Bunte Blätter, op. 36 (1899)

These 9 *kleine Stücke* (nine little pieces) are obviously not intended for the technically advanced player. Published originally in two volumes, they all have suggestive titles taken from the vast repertoire of terms used for romantic character pieces: *Humoreske* (no. 1), *Albumblatt* (no. 2), *Capriccietto* (no. 3), *Reigen* (no. 4), *Gigue* (no. 5), *Elegie* (no. 6), *Valse-Impromptu* (no. 7), *Capriccio* (no. 8), and *Rêverie* (no. 9).

They are again of a widely varying compositional quality. In some, Reger the efficient craftsman uses economized formal principles and arrives at balanced little musical entities (notably nos. 2, 3, and 6) similar to those well known *Kleinigkeiten* (ditties), as Robert Schumann called his *Kinderszenen*, op. 15. In others either stylistic (no. 8) or structural (no. 5) weaknesses are obvious, while the rest might be described as nondescript, ordinary compositions without specific merit. For the less advanced piano student nos. 1 and 2 might well serve as good teaching pieces, although the latter contains a few bars with awkward stretches for the left hand. Nos. 2 and 6 could even be included in recitals as challenging material for the talented younger student. It might be of interest to scrutinize one pertinent example from this set.

Op. 36, no. 1, *Humoreske*

As a concise and effective composition in the usual A–B–A form, this piece contains all the idiosyncratic traits which we by now associate with a *Humoreske* by Max Reger. The formal proportions are balanced and the phrase lengths surprisingly regular, the exception being the interjection bar 31, which delineates a transition. The texture and the inherent figurational characteristics seem to foreshadow Reger's later, more transparent writing. The principle of continuous variation of recurring figuration goes hand-in-hand with intensification of sonorities by octave doubling combined with contrasting dynamic changes. This can be seen clearly by comparing mm. 1–4, mm. 40–43, and mm. 79–82.

EXAMPLE 49A.   Op. 36, no. 1, mm. 1–4

EXAMPLE 49B.   Op. 36, no. 1, mm. 40–43

It is of utmost importance that the performer see the ingenious and often surprising dynamic fluctuations as an inherent part of the varied figuration and follow all indications meticulously.

In the shorter middle part, Reger employs his usual polyphonic texture and emphasizes the melodic line by adding the lower octave. Such a compositional procedure, when exploited to the extreme (note the climax of the fugue in op. 81), creates the compact sonorities considered another characteristic trademark of Reger's compositional grammar. Nevertheless, this impeccably crafted piece is of considerable pedagogical value for a maturing student, who is confronted by a beneficial array of technical and musical problems. In particular, the extremely diversified articulation (such as having both legato and staccato in one hand, mm. 73–77) and the required emphasis on the inner voice through figurative exchanges between the two hands (see mm. 84–86, or mm. 91–93 in Example 50) serve to expand the student's technical skills. The voice leading in the middle section can be an additional challenge, since it is necessary to emphasize the longer tied-over notes in order to elucidate the harmonic steps. The final cadence in the form of a Neapolitan progression is very characteristic of Reger.

♪ *Continues on following page.*

EXAMPLE 50.   Op. 36, no. 1, mm. 89–95

MIDDLE PERIOD

As previously mentioned, the rationale for the inclusion of opp. 44, 45, and 53 (composed in 1900) under the generally accepted heading "Munich Period" (which actually began in 1901) lies in the perception that various stylistic elements in those works point increasingly to the future. Of course, the distinction is as difficult to make as that pertaining to the characteristic stylistic elements of Beethoven's piano sonatas in what are generally defined as his early and middle periods. It would be preposterous to claim that a certain delineating date could be set in either case. The evolution of style within the oeuvres of both composers must be considered an organic continuum similar to the growth of a plant.

Zehn kleine Vortragsstücke, op. 44 (1900)
Similar to the *Humoresken*, op. 20, these "ten little performance pieces" constitute an artistic entity and could well be performed as such. They are

Title page of the first edition of the "Zehn kleine Vortragsstücke. . . ." op. 44, 1900. (Max Reger Institut)

carefully designed small masterpieces that combine substantial musical ideas with economical compositional means. Here Max Reger has discarded or transformed stylistic formulas influenced by the virtuosic romantic piano technique, including some of the dazzling mannerisms prevalent in the Lisztian School and the overloaded sonorities predominantly inspired by textures used by Brahms.

Instead, Reger has crafted ten musically concentrated gems that are permeated by subtle chromaticisms, highly sophisticated articulation, exquisitely balanced dynamic contrasts, and focused textural elements. Everything seems to evolve naturally and logically from imaginative musical ideas. This is unmistakably the language of a master. It is therefore the more surprising that Reger looked at these pieces with mixed feelings, cautiously adding the subtitle *Zum Gebrauche beim Unterricht* (For Teaching Purposes).[14]

There is no doubt, however, that this set of pieces represents a substantial compositional accomplishment, equally suitable as teaching material and as potentially successful performance pieces. It is certainly possible to include the whole set as a program point in a public recital. Even more successful could be various selections of smaller groups of three to five contrasting pieces. The titles follow the path already encountered in previous sets: *Albumblatt* (no. 1), *Burletta* (no. 2), *Es war einmal* (no. 3), *Capriccio* (no. 4), *Moment musical* (no. 5), *Scherzo* (no. 6), *Humoreske* (no. 7), *Fughette* (no. 8), *Gigue* (no. 9), and *Capriccio* (no. 10).

Although it would be worthwhile to discuss all ten pieces, a limited selection based on contrasting characteristics will have to suffice.

Op. 44, no. 3, *Es war einmal*

Not only the title but also the general mood of this piece points to Schumann, although Reger does not explicitly rely on similar compositional procedures. On the contrary, the haunting chromaticisms in the polyphonized harmony of the A section are in Reger's own idiosyncratic language and as such unsurpassed in their beauty. The balanced scheme of regular phrase lengths is contrasted strongly by the very active cross rhythms of the lively, short middle section. This conflict is amicably resolved by the recurrence of the A' section modified by the ever so subtle addition of chromatic passing notes, a good example of Reger's mastery in changing rather conventional harmonic progressions nearly imperceptibly into a distant key without the slightest inkling of artificiality.

Mäßig langsam und ausdrucksvoll

Op. 44, no. 5, *Moment Musical*

This charming musical moment contains in a nutshell important compositional features of Max Reger. Every young piano student could benefit from an acquaintance with this piece. The clearly indicated dynamic shadings alone require focused attention and should be clearly characterized. One example among many is provided by mm. 32–44.

EXAMPLE 52.   Op. 44, no. 5, mm. 32–44

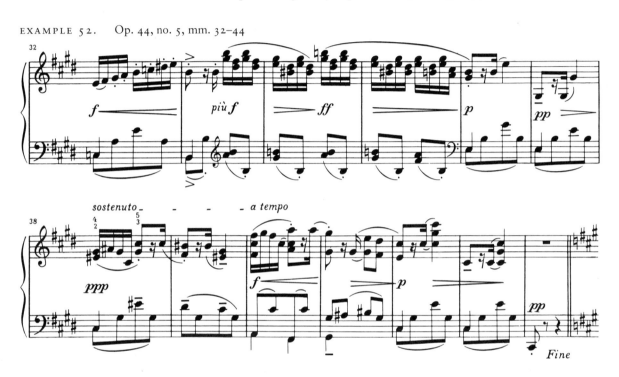

Although important, the intrinsic meaning of such differentiated dynamic indications reveals itself only when seen as integrated in a larger context that includes articulation, agogic accents, and phrasing as complementary ingredients.

The irregular phrase lengths are of particular interest, since they contribute largely to the floating character of the piece demanded by the indication *anmutig, etwas lebhaft, doch nicht zu sehr* (graceful, somewhat lively, but not too much). Frequently an interjection bar reiterates the last bar of a phrase which in itself might be irregular (see mm. 36–37 in Example 52). Reger frequently uses this particular compositional feature to avoid any possible "squareness." The horizontal perimeters of the musical flow are thus favourably expanded. In *Moment Musical* he uses this charming feature in mm. 10, 17, 22, 37, 53, and 58. These interjections, which often take the character of an echo, must be played with a special gesture as a sort of "overstated understatement."

Op. 44, no. 7, *Humoreske*

A vigorous pulsation of two beats per bar subdivided into strongly emphasized eighth note steps with highly articulated pairs of sixteenth notes serves as a strong rhythmic continuum in this powerful piece.

EXAMPLE 53.   Op. 44, no. 7, mm. 1–7

A comparison of the articulation patterns found in measures 12, 13, 14, 17, 22, and 24 in the following example reveals a surprising variety of interesting transformations.

EXAMPLE 54. Op. 44, no. 7, mm. 12–24

It is important to observe faithfully the minute details down to the difference between staccato dots and stroke signs in order to do justice to this brilliant character piece, which is one of the strongest in this set and perfectly suited for performance.

Op. 44, no. 10, *Capriccio*

As a pinnacle of dynamic contrasts, differentiated articulation, and rhythmical surprises, this piece exemplifies Reger's mastery in moulding short motifs of varying lengths into organic entities in a way which one might call "synthesis by contrast." The meter is only an ordering factor and has no bearing on the rhythm, which is basically determined by the character of the main motif in all its modifications.

EXAMPLE 55.   Op. 44, no. 10, mm. 1–2 and mm. 4–5

♪ *Continues on following page.*

The descending staccato line of the motif constitutes the unifying element. In conjunction with strategically placed chords the articulation clearly enhances the strong rhythmical propensities of this piece. The *capriccio* character is particularly obvious in the two dynamically and texturally contrasting "interjection phrases," mm. 11–13 and mm. 24–26.

EXAMPLE 56.   Op. 44, no. 10, mm. 24–26

One cannot imagine a more effective finale for this outstanding set of character pieces.

Sechs Intermezzi, op. 45 (1900)

Max Reger obviously designed these substantial virtuosic pieces with a particular performer in mind, the Viennese pianist Ella Kerndl. The formal, harmonic, and textural dimensions are generally extensive. The hypertrophy of texture and sound enshrouds more than enhances the basic musical ideas exposed in the beginning of the pieces. Reger wants too much and therefore "pulls all the stops." Many of the great composers he adored, of course, did the same, but obviously not as a means in itself, which cannot be but self-defeating. With this kind of compositional overkill, Reger calls his own artistic credibility into question. Not only the general expressiveness becomes excessive, but also the technical demands placed on the pianist, as is obvious in the following example, which is to be played "as fast as possible."

EXAMPLE 57.　Op. 45, no. 4, mm. 39–44

Many features point to the "Wild Munich Period" still to come, as represented by his *Violinsonate*, op. 72. The overblown virtuosic texture of most of the pieces is based mainly on the well-known formulas of the so-called Lisztian School and is often not commensurate with the given musical ideas. Only one piece, the *Intermezzo*, op. 45, no. 5, can reasonably be recommended for public performance.

♪ *Continues on following page.*

Op. 45, no. 5, *Intermezzo* (*Mit großer Leidenschaft und Energie*)
Reger again presents himself in his compositional procedures as a self-appointed heir to the passionate side of Brahms, expecting from the performer emotional expansiveness and boundless energy. After a first outburst (mm. 1–3), an evolution of convincing melodic and harmonic concepts takes place. Within a formal context of A–B–A'–B' the A section is dominated by harmony, while the more meditative B section beginning at m. 20 places considerable emphasis on melodic substance.

EXAMPLE 58.   Op. 45, no. 5, mm. 24–28

The sometimes heavy chordal writing in the A section leads to several substantial dynamic climaxes that contrast with the somber melodic lines of the B section, the later transformation of which incorporates extensive colouring by chromatically descending chord cascades reminiscent of Liszt's *Mazeppa*.

EXAMPLE 59.   Op. 45, no. 5, mm. 46–49

These sound waves create a mixture of harmonic support and colour somewhat distant from the noble character of the original melodic line. Nevertheless, the boldness of invention and the *grande pathétique* character give
this piece an intrinsic value.

♪ *Continues on following page.*

Silhouetten, op. 53 (1900)

A silhouette usually reveals the characteristic shape of a person or object in the form of an outline, without revealing inner details. Transforming this idea into music was one of Reger's ingenious creative accomplishments. We know that he very often made instinctive or deliberate use of the stylistic models of other composers. The concept of a whole set of pieces representing such models seems therefore quite natural for Max Reger, who intentionally presents the models of others in a manner uniquely his own. Gerhard Wünsch describes the stylistic essence of these pieces as "a loosening of the romantic-harmonic piano style towards . . . a highly personalized way of writing."[15]

Not all the pieces of op. 53 are clearly delineated silhouettes of recognizable features of other composers. With some measure of conjecture, however, one could say that the compositions numbered 2, 3, 4, and 5 appear to be stylistically related to Brahms, Grieg, Liszt, and Chopin, respectively. Although musical concepts seem to be derived from those models, Reger the craftsman uses them more as inspirational impulses. In spite of some quotations and closely copied stylistic features, one has to admire the composer's originality. These character pieces can be rated among the musically and technically most convincing works of the so-called "Weiden Period." It is therefore not surprising that these *Silhouetten* have always been extremely popular with amateur pianists. Occasionally they even appear in concerts. Since op. 53, no. 1, could be considered a silhouette of Max Reger himself, it might be sufficient to discuss only that and the Brahmsian no. 2.

Op. 53, *Silhouette,* no. 1

One can immediately recognize the now mature burlesque style as Max Reger's own idiosyncratic expression and contribution to piano literature.

EXAMPLE 60.   Op. 53, no. 1, mm. 1–3

The texture is very transparent, the strongly articulated figurations imaginative, and the dynamics exquisitely differentiated, full of surprising contrasts. In addition, the changes of register are skilfully employed, and some special effects are incorporated as well (see m. 44). The formal aspects are quite conventional and follow the customary ternary pattern: A(a–b–a)–B–A'(a'–b'–a')–coda. As usual, Reger continuously increases the density of the texture and the vivacity of the figurative patterns, but this time in a most economical and meaningful way. The light character of the fast-moving piece is thus maintained throughout. The characteristic ingredients of Reger's "textural music" are all present, including constantly varied short motifs, strong articulation contrasts, and an infinite variety of dynamics.

It seems that in this type of music, harmony and melody constitute approximately one-third of the overall compositional weight, while articulation as a means of rhythmic diversification and varied dynamics represent the other two-thirds. One could call this a "threefold equality" of compositional means in Max Reger's music. Other features like tempo changes and the use of the pedal seem to be quite subservient to these main compositional pillars.

Because of the implied tempo, the performer faces considerable technical challenges, especially when abrupt register changes are requested.

EXAMPLE 61.   Op. 53, no. 1, mm. 48–52

The execution of some of the "tricky" spots can be facilitated by an intelligent division of the texture between both hands. A performer commanding a mature technical mastery might enjoy playing this *Silhouette* as an intriguing example of the Regerian burlesque style.

Op. 53, *Silhouette*, no. 2

The build-up (or build-down) of a harmony from above, which happens twice in the beginning of this piece, is strongly reminiscent of op. 119, no. 1, by Johannes Brahms, an *Intermezzo* in the same key and meter. It is fascinating to observe the obvious ease with which Max Reger incorporated a characteristic melodic shape or structural concept of another composer without any obvious intent of plagiarism. In this respect he must have seen himself as simply using baroque compositional procedures in which such "borrowings" were quite acceptable.

EXAMPLE 62.   Brahms, op. 119, no. 1, mm. 1–4

EXAMPLE 63.   Op. 53, no. 2, mm. 1–4

There are many similarities in texture (Reger's mm. 9–10 and Brahms's mm. 4 and 6) and even in the way triplets are used (Reger's mm. 12 and 14 and Brahms's mm. 47 and 48). Max Reger has by now consolidated his own harmonic, textural, and melodic language (in that order) to such an extent that the obvious reminiscences of a specific piece by Brahms appear transformed and amalgamated, in much the same way that Bartók assimilated stylistic features of East European folk cultures.

This piece is especially instructive in a pedagogical sense, since Reger envisages an immaculate legato playing similar to that required for playing the organ. The challenge for the performers lies in the transference of idiosyncratic organ fingerings to the piano in combination with an intelligent use of the pedal.

EXAMPLE 64.   Op. 53, no. 2, mm. 29–31

At the same time, the player must listen carefully to the dynamic weight of specific notes within the harmonic structure. The subsequent pedal changes clear the way for the tied-over notes, which very often serve as a suspension. The piece should be performed with as much finger legato as possible, since the tactile sense acts as a physiological stimulant, enhancing one's understanding of the voice leading. It is again apparent how much Reger's linear, polyphonic thinking is based on his allegiance to the organ as the classic instrument for polyphonic structures.

Zehn Klavierstücke, op. 79a (1901–1903)

The origin of this collection was a request by the publisher Ernst Rabich for continuous contributions in the form of smaller character pieces for his periodical, *Blätter für Haus- und Kirchenmusik*. A unifying thought comparable to that in op. 53 therefore does not exist in this heterogeneous collection. Since Reger subjected himself to considerable restrictions with respect to his usually overloaded texture, these pieces, although by no means easy, are readily accessible to the advanced younger piano student and talented amateur.

While the collection as a whole is not as consistent in compositional quality as the *Silhouetten*, the following pieces are worthwhile contributions to the literature, in particular with regard to their pedagogical value: *Humoreske II* (no. 2), *Intermezzo* (no. 3), *Romanze* (no. 5), *Caprice* (no. 8), and *Capriccio* (no. 9). In addition, one could consider no. 9 an effective encore piece for a concert program. The titles of the other pieces are *Humoreske I* (no. 1), *Melodie* (no. 4), *Impromptu* (no. 6), *Impromptu (Studie)* (no. 7), and *Melodie* (no. 10). It is interesting to observe that in no. 7, which carries the subtitle "study," Max Reger seems to be working according to a model taken from Chopin's *Études*, op. 10, and mixing it with other, mainly rhythmical, stylistic elements found in Chopin's *Études* in general. In addition, no. 7 seems to be an outgrowth of musical concepts underlying no. 6.

EXAMPLE 65.   Op. 79a, no. 7, mm. 1–2

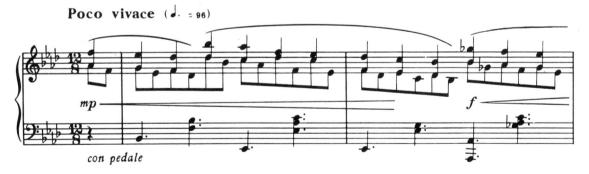

Again, quite a number of seemingly derivative stylistic features of masters like Schumann, Chopin, Mendelssohn, and Brahms overshadow Reger's own idiosyncratic handwriting, which surfaces only occasionally, as, for instance, in the typical harmonic progression in the coda of no. 6.

EXAMPLE 66.   Op. 79a, no. 6, mm. 46–51

Of the five pieces suitable for teaching purposes on a more advanced level, three pieces representing different compositional elements require closer attention.

Op. 79a, no. 3, *Intermezzo*
The continuous and seemingly stereotypical application of one single rhythmical pattern in the form of a syncopated figure within a 3/8 note pulsation throughout the main A or A' sections is counterbalanced by rather bold harmonic progressions shaped in quite irregular phrases. If one compares this piece with Brahms's *Capriccio*, op. 116, no. 1, which is based on a similar rhythmical concept, it is obvious that by avoiding any firm reference to a clearly delineated conventional formal structure, Max Reger creates that particular flowing horizontal motion so characteristic of many of his passionate pieces. It seems inappropriate to evaluate the formal concepts inherent in this piece only on the basis of those found in the piece by Brahms, who followed different formal principles altogether.

EXAMPLE 67.   Brahms, op. 116, no. 1, mm. 1–6

Still, in using the syncopated split harmonies, Reger, like Brahms, creates a strong forward propulsion which is maintained throughout the
piece, with the exception of a rather short chordal middle section.

EXAMPLE 68.   Op. 79a, no. 3, mm. 1–16

In the embellished return of the A section, Max Reger's mastery of subjecting formal proportions to the necessity of harmonic logic is evident. The dominant chord in m. 110 requests a solution to the tonic which is available in the third bar of the original 8 bar phrase. Thus the first two bars have simply been omitted, shortening the phrase to six bars.

EXAMPLE 69.   Op. 79a, no. 3, mm. 111–116

The figurative metamorphosis of a basic idea is harmonically varied and formally changed by substantial omissions (the expected formal equivalents of mm. 17–26 and mm. 44–50 are omitted at m. 124 and m. 139, respectively). These fascinating proportional twists, in combination with the unusual harmonic progressions and imaginatively varied figuration, render this piece a worthwhile addition to the teaching repertoire of the more enterprising piano teacher.

Op. 79a, no. 5, *Romanze*

A beautifully meandering melodic line of irregular phrase lengths (11 and 13 bars) is set in the well-known "tenor melody" style found in Mendelssohn's *Songs without Words*. This type of texture contributes to a dreamlike expression commensurate with the title.

EXAMPLE 70. Op. 79a, no. 5, mm. 57–69

It is clear that an ingenious concept of harmonic logic created and shaped this expanded melodic line. One could even imagine the first nine bars constituting a fugue theme similar to those long entities found in op. 81 or op. 134. Some seemingly erratic interjections (as in mm. 36 ff. or mm. 97 ff.) lead to an obviously intended instability or ambiguity strongly determined by harmonic factors.

EXAMPLE 71.   Op. 79a, no. 5, mm. 97–101

With respect to formal proportions, it is difficult to accept as musically logical the in itself quite charming F sharp major bridge between the two main sections. Rhythmically destabilized, this extremely short introverted section can only be considered an aphorism within this context. It is simply overwhelmed by the musical weight of the following embellished, modified, and somewhat transformed A' part with its expansive climax.

Max Reger increasingly shapes the formal aspects of his music not according to conventional architectonic principles, but based on his own feeling for organic growth and emotional flow expressed in harmonic motion. Therefore, the question arises whether the written text really represents the totality of the work or whether the "improvisatory" side of any live performance might have to be envisaged as an intangible ingredient of every composition (see also Chapter 5). According to Cadenbach, the text as such is not the "work . . . but only the way to it."[16]

Op. 79a, no. 9, *Capriccio*

In this piece, the perpetual, some might say excessive, focus on small motivic groups as building blocks is ingeniously combined with continuous sequential treatment. The various musical ideas are loosely intertwined, the first being dominant and acting as a unifying element in the A and A' sections.

EXAMPLE 72.   Op. 79a, no. 9, mm. 1–4

The B section, set in a low register, provides a short respite quite evocative in its harmonic and melodic design. With the exception of some added figuration, A' is identical with A and followed by one of Reger's characteristic final statements.

♪ *Continues on following page.*

EXAMPLE 73.   Op. 79a, no. 9, mm. 114–123

This is a very effective, playful example of the burlesque type and has considerable pedagogical value, in particular with regard to figuration and articulation.

Variationen und Fuge über ein Thema von J.S. Bach, op. 81 (1904)

The *Bach Variations*, op. 81, are the first of a succession of substantial variation works which subsequently also embraced the media of two pianos (opp. 86 and 96) and the orchestra (opp. 100 and 132). Even the strongest critics of Reger's "compositional megalomania" will concede that with the *Bach Variations* the composer created a work of significant magnitude and deep musical substance. In addition, many admirers are convinced that for this work alone the composer would deserve a place in the musical Valhalla reserved for great masters such as Bach, Beethoven, and Brahms.

In his formal, technical, and spiritual scope, Max Reger continues and in some ways transcends the great tradition of variation writing established by Beethoven, who focused on a concentrated dissection of rather simplis-

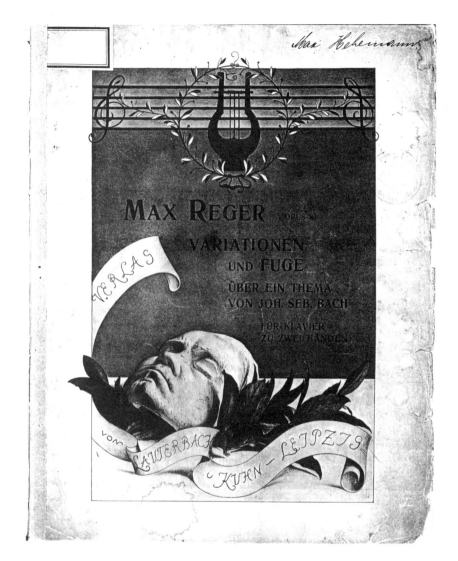

Title page of the first edition
of the *Bach-Variations,*
op. 81, 1904. (Max Reger
Institut)

tic thematic material in his *Diabelli Variations,* op. 120; Schumann, who
indulged in free, imaginative character variations in his *Études Symphoniques,* op. 13; and Brahms, who combined baroque features with an
expanded romantic melos in his *Handel Variations,* op. 24. Like these
works, which extended existing conventions through new compositional
features, Reger's *Bach Variations* further enlarged these dimensions within

the perimeters of this basic and oldest musical form. As might be expected, these expansions are mainly centred around harmonic concepts and procedures, but are also obvious in the various ways the composer treated texture in combination with dynamics. Most important, however, is the substantial growth of the varied exploitation of the thematic material along the lines of Schumann's model and the extensive combination of homophonic and polyphonic textures.

The *Bach Variations* can be considered Reger's most genuine musical utterance for solo piano. They reveal his compositional mastery in a most idiosyncratic way, amalgamating many stylistic models which so often permeated his previous works. Some scholars have specifically commented on Reger's vast expansion of the treatment of the motivic variation, in which any perceivable affinity to the theme disappears altogether.[17]

In this creation Reger has found his genuine musical language, which was accepted with great enthusiasm by pianists of his time. It may be said that without this particular enthusiasm as a necessary spiritual powerhouse, no pianist who dares to face the inherent technical and musical difficulties will be able to render a successful performance of this major work. The historic first performance by August Schmid-Lindner in Munich, December 14, 1904, was an undisputed success and Max Reger's already growing reputation was now firmly established.

The variations are based on a theme taken from the *Cantata BWV 128*, "Auf Christi Himmelfahrt allein ich meine Nachfahrt gründe." The choice of such a theme might indicate that Reger "envisaged a music that could not follow any more the traditional categories of the variation form."[18] The 14-bar theme appears in the obbligato part of the oboe d'amore before and after the alto and tenor duet. Its melodic shape of rise and fall encompasses multiple harmonic possibilities, recognized and exploited by Reger to the fullest. The proportions of the theme are delineated by three sections of six, four, and four bars, which in themselves provide enough motivic material to enable Reger to use the given melodic line not only as a whole, but also in parts as an inspirational source, similar to Beethoven's procedures in his op. 120.

EXAMPLE 74. Op. 81, theme

1) *Ich bitte, alle Metronomangaben als nicht strikte bindend anzusehen; doch dürften die Metronomangaben besonders bei den beweg-ten (schnellen) Variationen und hauptsächlich bei der Fuge, der ein breites Tempo immer gelegen sein wird, als die überhaupt höchst zu-lässigen Tempi in bezug auf „Schnelligkeit" gelten, wenn nicht der Vortrag auf Kosten der Deutlichkeit leiden soll.*

The rather awkwardly stated footnote visible at the bottom of Example 74 can be translated as follows: "I ask that all the metronome markings not be considered strictly binding; however, especially in the fast variations and mainly in the fugue, in which a broader tempo is always fitting, the metronome markings should always be considered the maximum allowable tempi with respect to 'speed,' so that the performance does not suffer any loss of clarity."[19]

The *sempre assai legato* statement of the theme is carefully harmonized in four-part writing, and the doubling of the bass already points towards a texture usually associated with the organ. Reger himself did not number the variations, although all except the second end on a *fermata* written over either the last note or the last bar line. The emotional content seems to indicate that Reger conceived the work as a continuum, thereby reflecting in a romantic way a stylistic trait of the baroque era.

It is safe to assume that in the beginning of this monumental work Max Reger intended to focus the listener's attention on the rather long theme. Thus he restricts himself in the first two variations to figurative elaborations of the melodic line in a polyphonic texture based on the original harmonic scheme. His technique of incorporating more and more passing notes inevitably builds up to the well-known "chordal condensations" that culminate in combination with strong dynamics at the end of the second variation in dense Regerian sonorities.

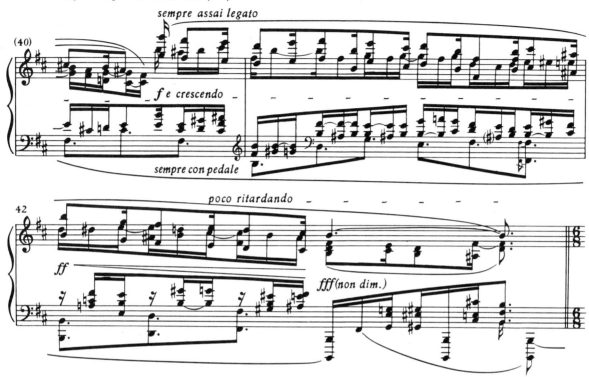

EXAMPLE 75.   Op. 81, var. 2, mm. 40–42

The consistency with which Reger indicates minutely tied-over notes in the inner voices presents a formidable challenge to the performer, who must create the impression of a logical continuum of constantly evolving harmonic progressions. Technically, this means, first, a dynamic emphasis on the notes that are tied over and thus a functional part of each following harmony and, second, a continuous but subtle application of the sustaining pedal.

While the theme in the first two variations is retained as a whole, it is broken up in the third variation as an indication of the general way in which Max Reger intends to treat the theme, namely, as a source of inspiration from which musical ideas and motifs emerge in the composer's creative process. It is therefore quite legitimate to call this variation a fantasy on motifs from the theme and to expect the performer to treat it with that particular improvisatory freedom associated with a fantasy.

EXAMPLE 76. Op. 81, var. 3, mm. 43–44

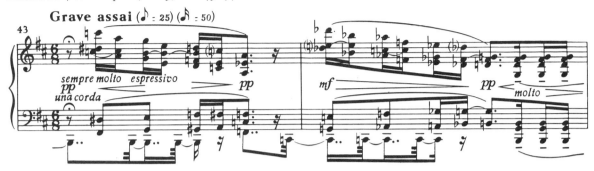

The multitude of expressive indicators is surprising. In addition, the tempo indications, including exact metronome markings, change with nearly every bar. The question arises whether a slavish adherence to this type of exactness does not stifle any creative interpretation of such highly individualized music. One should not forget Reger's own comments, in which he suggests that all metronome markings are to be taken with a "grain of salt" and considered maximum tempi, especially in the faster variations and in the fugue (see note 19 in this chapter). The proliferation of figuration sometimes grows into so-called "mammoth bars," which then appear like graphically eloquent pictures of Reger's hypertrophic figurations.

EXAMPLE 77. Op. 81, var. 3, m. 49

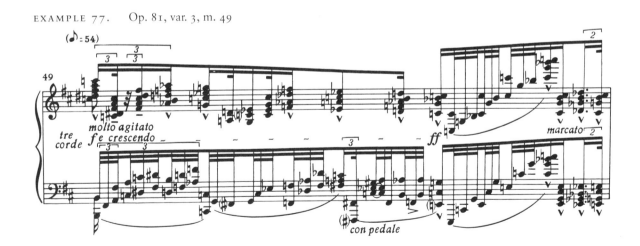

Variations 4 and 5 are textural in concept. While variation 4 retains the basic harmonic scheme and formal proportions of the theme, variation 5 uses the melodic contours of the first bars of the theme as a germ cell for continuous growth, thereby expanding the formal boundaries considerably. (Note the seamless change from 6/8 to a 9/8 bar in m. 79, shown in Example 79.) Variation 4 explores the exchange of hands, resulting in some intriguing, often chromatic, inner lines with the characteristic thumb exchange.

EXAMPLE 78.   Op. 81, var. 4, m. 68

Seamlessly interlocking arm motions are essential in any interpretation in order to arrive at the smooth, fluent continuum clearly suggested by the notation.

Variation 5 is determined by orchestral concepts. Pulsating staccato chords suggest woodwinds in fast repetition and offer a technical challenge to the performer, especially when legato in one hand complements staccato in the other.

♪ *Continues on following page.*

EXAMPLE 79.   Op. 81, var. 5, mm. 78–79

The fast repeating octave patterns can easily cause muscular stiffness in even a technically advanced player and must be intelligently counteracted. It might be advisable to change the angle of the hand continuously within each group of three sixteenth notes and aim for an overall relaxed flexibility of the arm according to the hand position on either black or white keys.

A change of meter and the abundant virtuosic figurations based on concepts developed by Liszt give variation 6 a strongly contrasting character. Indications like *ben marcato il Tema* or *ben marcato ed espressivo la melodia* draw the attention to various splinters of thematic material which the performer must emphasize in an intelligently differentiated way, since the composer uses a variety of articulation signs within the same context (including staccato 𝅘𝅥 , stroke sign 𝅘𝅥 , tenuto line 𝅘𝅥 , accent 𝅘𝅥 , staccato dot with tenuto line 𝅘𝅥 , and stroke sign with accent 𝅘𝅥).

A welcome release from all the previous virtuosic tension is found in variation 7, an introverted *adagio* variation that employs mystical-sounding, bold harmonic progressions and incorporates the end of the theme in the last three bars.

EXAMPLE 80.   Op. 81, var. 7, mm. 125–127

Here the famous "velvet touch" of Reger the pianist should be the aim of the interpreter, who must be able to relinquish any physical edginess and psychological tension whatsoever.

As a striking contrast to the previous variation, in variation 8 changes of key, tempo, dynamics, and rhythm are reminiscent of procedures encountered in Schumann's *Études Symphoniques*, op. 13. It is essentially non-thematic, although the first five steps in the bass line could possibly be associated with the theme. The interpretive musical and technical challenges lie in the constant cross-rhythms created by figurations that seem to negate the inherent 6/8 pulsation. (Note again the expansion of the meter to 9/8 in m. 130.)

EXAMPLE 81.   Op. 81, var. 8, mm. 128–130

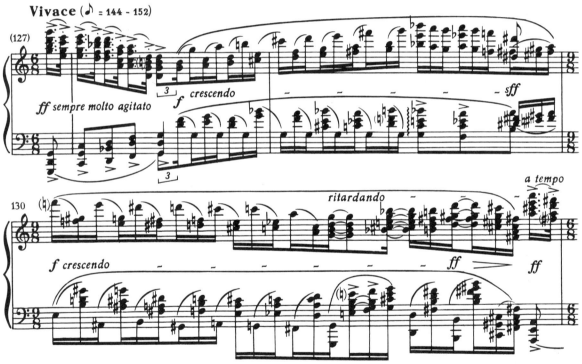

Variation 9 provides another extreme contrast by changing to the tonic *maggiore* key (B major) and emphasizing the *dolcissimo*, *legato*, and *tempo rubato* character. The time signature (18/16) suggests a slow pace for the almost impressionistic chord progressions that support an endless melodic line to be delineated with *delicatezza* by the grace notes (see Example 82), which might be most efficiently realized by letting an apparently weightless relaxed right hand drop tenderly onto the key.

EXAMPLE 82.   Op. 81, var. 9, m. 146

In variations 10 and 11 Reger returns to a renewed exploration of pianistic figurations, centred around expansive octave lines in variation 10 and broken chords combined with cross rhythms in variation 11, in which meter and key also change. In variation 10 it is necessary for the performer to embrace the long sweeping bass lines as the basis for an uninterrupted continuum, while 11 presents challenges similar to those found in variation 8.

♪ *Continues on following page.*

As a further respite, Reger adds as variation 12 an intimate *andante sostenuto*, in which he quotes a portion of the theme in mm. 211 ff. The requested generous application of the pedal—"*ma delicato*[!]"—predicates a thorough understanding of the complex harmonic structure, as clearly indicated, for instance, by the differentiated note values in the various broken chord figurations.

EXAMPLE 83.   Op. 81, var. 12, mm. 206–208

An extraordinary contrast to the preceding intimacy, variation 13 displays a healthy predilection for brilliant pianism. A number of varied and articulated figurative patterns, including virtuosic *martellato* chord exchanges between both hands, constitute a formidable task for the performing pianist. There is a risk that the massive chords in *fff* will become merely ponderous; a strong emphasis on the treble and bass contours can make the chordal avalanche less oppressive and help to avoid this problem, while preserving the piece's powerful impact.

EXAMPLE 84.   Op. 81, var. 13, mm. 236–240

♪ *Continues on following page.*

The final variation before the fugue displays for the last time the whole theme *ff* in octaves and chords, set in the lower register. The massive chordal elaborations in the treble register incorporate the characteristic "articulation figuration" (two sixteenth notes legato, two sixteenth notes staccato), pointing already to the basic articulation of the second theme of the fugue, which shows the same figurative pattern.

EXAMPLE 85.   Op. 81, var. 14, mm. 241–242

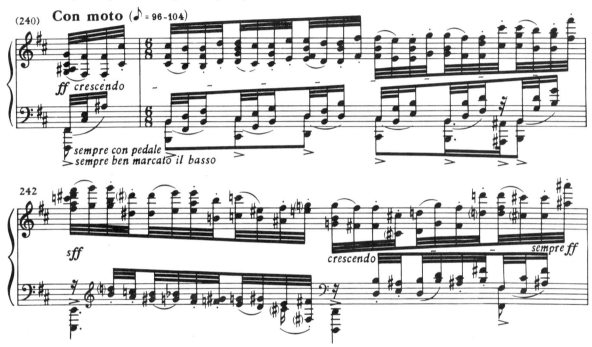

Towards the end the inner texture is increasingly filled with harmonic material, resulting in an overwhelming mass of sound. Such a gigantic climax on a grand piano could only be surpassed by the *tutti* sound of a huge organ in a cathedral. Again, the performer is cautioned not to use absolutely every dynamic resource possible on a modern piano. The inherent danger of substituting vulgarity for nobility of expression should not be underestimated.

The fugue is designed as a double fugue with an intensely melodious first theme moving within an astonishingly wide ambitus. In order to shape this fourfold phrased melody successfully, a performer must express the growing tension created by the increasing intervals (from a fourth to a seventh) with commensurate agogic gestures.

EXAMPLE 86.   Op. 81, fugue, mm. 255–258

The exposition is in four voices, carried through in strict counterpoint to a *caesura* before the second theme is exposed in a similar but formally modified manner.

♪ *Continues on following page.*

EXAMPLE 87.　Op. 81, fugue, mm. 333–337

Reger typically introduces his fugue themes in the utmost *pianissimo* followed by a subsequent perpetual increase of the dynamic level. This strategy anticipates a continuous process of growth from a nearly imperceptible beginning towards an overwhelmingly massive ending, thus allowing for a welcome emotional breathing space after the climax of the last variation. The spacing of the dynamic increase is perhaps one of the greatest challenges pianists face in this fugue, or for that matter in all final fugues of Reger's variation works for the piano.[20]

Reger continuously increases all parameters in this fugue, first by beginning to present the re-entry of the first theme (m. 327) in octaves, then intensifying the continuous motion by using increasingly the figurative pattern of the second theme in all voices.

EXAMPLE 88.   Op. 81, fugue, mm. 347–348

Successive chordal thickening and motivic *strettos* build up tension towards a super-massive final climax, in which the beginning of the first theme is presented *marcatissimo* and supported by chordal sound patterns in triple *fortissimo*. A continuous broadening of the pace towards the final statement in quadruple *fortissimo* exhausts all the emotional resources of the performer as well as the listener.

EXAMPLE 89.   Op. 81, fugue, mm. 380–384

Although such an overwhelming expressionistic statement is not easily digested in our time, in which spiritual concepts are far removed from the emotional indulgences found in the exalted musical language of Max Reger, this work will always hold its own as a superb masterpiece of the late romantic era.

Aus meinem Tagebuch, op. 82/I (1904)

Immediately after completing the *Bach Variations*, op. 81, Max Reger poured his "other musical soul" into these twelve character pieces as if he needed a relaxing counter-measure to his conquest of that summit of musical and pianistic accomplishment. A feeling of relaxation and the absence of any particular pressure either from within himself or from any of his publishers may have contributed to the superior quality of these eloquent pieces. Max Reger finally appears not as a feverishly determined mountain climber but as a true *homo ludens*, having either consciously or subconsciously prevented himself from overburdening this music with *Bedeutung* (meaning). He avoids any of his sometimes extreme dynamic and textural excesses, keeping the formal aspects concise and balanced, the overall size of each piece short and concentrated, and the texture more transparent than ever. The latter characteristic points to a new influence on his expressive aims. The increasing economy in his compositional technique is certainly a result of his intensified encounter with Mozart's music.

Reger also keeps figurative elaborations and the augmentation of sonorities in repeated passages to a manageable minimum, thereby creating healthy, well-balanced musical entities. As in op. 44, the compositional quality of all pieces is equally high. Thus it is not surprising that this collection was an immediate success with the piano-playing public—a fact that stimulated Reger later to add another three collections under the same opus number.

Since the lyrical, tender, "mood" pieces dominate the more boisterous, humorous, burlesque-type compositions, it might not be advisable to use the whole set in a public concert. It is doubtful that Max Reger would have endorsed such an idea, since there simply is not enough contrast to sustain the listener's interest. However, one can select any combination of four or five contrasting pieces as a successful part of a concert program. A suitably balanced combination would be nos. 3, 4, 6, and 9, or nos. 1, 11, 7, 12, and 9. Most of these compositions are equally useful as excellent teaching and concert pieces.

Five pieces have been somewhat arbitrarily selected for a more detailed discussion as the most characteristic samples, representing in some way most of the others, which are equally worth exploring.

Op. 82/I, no. 1 (*Vivace*)
From the very beginning, cross rhythms (3/4 versus 6/8) permeate this fast, vibrant, dance piece.

EXAMPLE 90.   Op. 82/I, no. 1, mm. 1–4

In comparison with similar earlier pieces, the texture is more transparent and the overall architectural proportions within the A–B–A–coda form extremely well-balanced—aspects that among others are indicative of Reger's continuously maturing style. The phrase structure is amazingly regular and facilitates immediate understanding. Typical of Max Reger is the deliberate veiling of the tonality in the very beginning (mm. 1–4), defining it only in m. 5. To do justice to this harmonically and rhythmically exquisite creation, it is paramount to avoid the danger of inadvertently changing the 6/8 pulse to twice 3/8, and to apply a light, feathery touch throughout, even in *forte* passages.

Op. 82/I, no. 3 (*Andante sostenuto*)
The eternal question regarding Reger's music as to whether the melody is determined by harmonic concepts or vice versa may never be conclusively answered. However, when both melody and harmony are presented in a delicate fusion as convincingly as in this beautiful gem, the question seems utterly irrelevant. The short two- or three-bar phrases of an enticing melodic line are transformed and harmonized in a continuous metamorphosis. A more lively triplet figuration is introduced in the middle section and later combined with the primary musical idea. This leads to a highly

unified structure in the last seven bars (mm. 35–41), culminating in a final climax in which melodic and rhythmical characteristics are intensely amalgamated.

EXAMPLE 91.   Op. 82/I, no. 3, mm. 35–41

Max Reger's mastery of modulation is obvious in this piece, which is particularly appropriate for teaching and performance. The detailed dynamic indications are to be followed to the letter, since they frequently are not congruent with the natural rise and fall of the melodic contours. One of the most characteristic traits of Reger's melodic concept (see Example 91) seems to be the release of dynamic tension before the apex of a melodic line is reached.

Op. 82/I, no. 4 (*Vivace*)
Here the combination of a fast pace in 6/8 with contrasting strongly articulated intervals is similar to that of the *Gigue*, op. 44, no. 4 (see Example 92), which could be considered a forerunner of this piece.

EXAMPLE 92.   Op. 44, no. 4, mm. 29–32

EXAMPLE 93. Op. 82/I, no. 4, mm. 42–47

Both pieces are built upon the principle of perpetual motion, with contrasting articulations and chromaticisms enlivening the typical Regerian sequence technique. Although separated by only four years, the later one shows far more depth and maturity and is also rhythmically more intricate. The realization of the incongruent slurring in the figurations in both hands requires a precise coordination of alternating physical motions.

The contrasting middle section with its extreme chromaticism and well-balanced form contributes considerably to the overall strength of this brilliant concert piece. The textural elements are in complete congruence with the underlying musical ideas.

♪ *Continues on following page.*

Op. 82/I, no. 9 (*Vivace*)

Although it is untitled, this piece is certainly a *burlesque par excellence.* In its economical design it is in no way overloaded like some of the earlier pieces in this genre. Many of the characteristic features of the Regerian *Burleske* are present, including the 2/4 meter and commensurate rhythmical structure, highly articulated staccato passages, the typical "articulation figuration," strong dynamic contrasts, melodic thumb exchanges (see mm. 90–91), and surprise off-beat accentuations (see mm. 18–21). The figurations are varied in a most imaginative way and the chromaticisms unobtrusively integrated. They are used never to thicken the melodic and harmonic flow, but to highlight the harmonic structure. Unlike other excellent virtuosic concert pieces, this ends in a witty *non ritardando pianissimo.*

EXAMPLE 94.   Op. 82/I, no. 9, mm. 102–105

Op. 82/I, no. 10 (*Andante innocente*)

A hauntingly simple melodic line supported by equally modest harmonic progressions represents the "innocent" character Reger envisaged.

EXAMPLE 95.   Op. 82/I, no. 10, mm. 1–5

This time the composer uses his chromatic language with a particularly subtle sensitivity, tastefully underlining the noble expressiveness of the A section. In spite or because of the irregularity of the phrase structure (5–3–3–4–4) and the short melodic motifs, a magic continuity emerges, interrupted and contrasted only by a short, more articulated *poco più mosso* with some burlesque characteristics. It is essential for a performer to connect the various phrases and phrase groupings by means of strong *rubato* inflections, tastefully applied. To play such music in a straightforward, objective, modern way would be destructive and self-defeating.

With added chromatic passing notes, the repeat of the A section appears even smoother, yet more melodious and linear, ending with a Neapolitan progression from the key of F to E extended over the last three bars (see Example 2). Reger uses such a formula quite a number of times for final cadences, providing an inimitable harmonic flavour. It seems only logical that this sublime piece concludes with just such an imaginative treatment.

Aus meinem Tagebuch, op. 82/II (1906)

The composition of the second volume of op. 82 was stimulated by the commercial success of the first collection two years earlier. The same stylistic aspects prevail. These *Zehn kleine Stücke* (ten small pieces) are generally short and in the usual A–B–A–coda form, although some, such as no. 8, are a little more extended. As was the case with some earlier collections, the compositional quality is uneven, ranging from the virtuosity and balance of a masterpiece such as no. 8 to the trivial imitation of Chopin's *Berceuse* in no. 9. Most pieces, however (notably no. 1 and no. 6), show solid craftsmanship and are sometimes quite evocative. Some provide good teaching material, acquainting students with the now mature piano style of Reger (no. 1) or particular technical idiosyncrasies (no. 3 and no. 5). Two pieces might be of particular interest: no. 5 reveals some of the salient imaginative and compositional processes of Reger's mature style, and no. 8 contains a number of pianistically interesting figurations and combinations of sound. Familiarity with these idiosyncrasies will have considerable bearing on the way one would interpret these particular pieces and, for that matter, Reger's piano music in general.

Op. 82/II, no. 5 (*Allegretto con grazia; sempre poco agitato*)

A good example of Reger's compositional procedures, this delicate, mosaic-like play with motifs and short sections of different figurative and rhythmical connotations seems to have flown naturally and effortlessly from the composer's imagination onto the manuscript. The musical building blocks are often related, interlocked, and modified in a most subtle fashion. Note, for instance, the various ascending and descending half-tone steps in the following examples:

Allegretto con grazia; sempre poco agitato ($\quarternote$=132-144)

EXAMPLE 96B.   Op. 82/II, no. 5, m. 24–25

EXAMPLE 96C.   Op. 82/II, no. 5, m. 30–33

♪ *Continues on following page.*

The main sections are clearly delineated (mm. 1 ff., 13 ff., 23 ff., and 36 ff.), then modified (m. 57) or altered (mm. 57 ff. and 68 ff.). In view of these constructive procedures, it is quite understandable that Reger was once called a "musical engineer" (see note 11, Chapter 3). An analysis of Reger's work procedures seems to support the existence of a "tendency of a totally unconcealed montage: bars and whole parts of a work are taken out and eliminated or inserted at another place."[21]

However, this must be considered a totally unconventional process of shaping form, a process that follows its own laws and should not necessarily be judged on the basis of the generally accepted *Formbildung* (creation of form). In this respect this piece is extremely useful in understanding Reger's creative process. The abundance of chromaticism is an essential compositional device, smoothing the harmonic steps in frequent modulations and sequences, as seen in the example below, which is representative of many others, including mm. 24 ff. and mm. 74 ff.

EXAMPLE 97. Op. 82/II, no. 5, mm. 32–35

The main task of the performer is, of course, to pay close attention to the intricate articulation, in particular the difference between staccato dots and stroke signs. For a rhythmically elastic execution of the varied articulated note values, a flexible wrist is an absolutely necessity.

Op. 82/II, no. 8 (*Vivacissimo*)
These 250 bars of brilliant pianistic writing incorporate extraordinary staccato patterns resulting in new, intriguing sonorities reminiscent of Richard Strauss, yet very much Reger's own. The variety of articulations, the fast interchange of hands, and the contrasting dynamics and changes of register radiate an exuberant vibrancy.

♪ *Continues on following page.*

EXAMPLE 98. Op. 82/II, no. 8, mm. 49–60

Reger's preference for the higher registers is conducive to many virtuosic cascades, when in *forte* or *fortissimo*, and to glittering sound effects similar to *glissando*, when in *pianissimo*.

EXAMPLE 99.   Op. 82/II, no. 8, mm. 32–35

The rather square modulatory middle section acts as a welcome respite before an expanded and modified A section concludes the work, demanding a splendid staccato technique to do justice to the tempo requested by the composer. This is an excellent concert piece for the advanced player, for whom listening to Max Reger playing his *Humoreske*, op. 20, no. 5, as recorded on the Welte-Mignon system in 1905, is a must. That recording reveals many essential interpretive characteristics (see note 11 in this chapter).

Aus meinem Tagebuch, op. 82/III (1911)
Aus meinem Tagebuch, op. 82/IV (1912)
The third and fourth collections of op. 82 are in no way comparable to the first or even the second set, but contain ordinary compositions with the usual titles of genre pieces, generally lacking the compositional mastery, scrutinizing care, and sense of inner participation so obvious in the first collection. Most of the pieces reflect a casual attitude and even give the impression that the composer considered them a necessary routine task in response to the demands of an insatiable public. The sometimes stunning discrepancies in quality in Max Reger's piano music give rise to questions as to the possible reasons for the domination of compositional craftsmanship over musical inspiration. Gerhard Wünsch even feels that in some of the late collections a "rational materialistic" influence replaces the intuitive imagination with routine and superior technique.[22] The genius of Max Reger seems to lie in his subconscious perception of musical ideas and forms which emerge into real consciousness only in the process of writing them down on paper. Whenever the composer applied his analytical mind to this process, substantial musical creations seemed to emerge in a natural

way. If that particular screening was weak or diminished, the ingenious subconscious activities seemed to follow their own paths. The results were often rather amorphous compositions that have interesting and sometimes even beautiful details, but fall short as entire artistic entities.

Op. 82/IV, no. 3, *Intermezzo*

This otherwise insignificant piece lends itself to an interesting experiment, which sheds some light on the ambiguity of Reger's harmonic concepts. Careful scrutiny of mm. 4–10 reveals that they could be interchanged without significantly altering the overall musical flow and harmonic logic.

EXAMPLE 100.   Op. 82/IV, no. 3, mm. 4–11

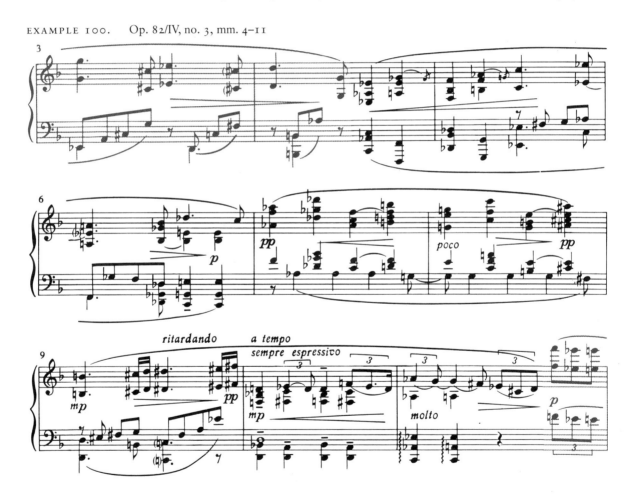

For instance, m. 9 could be inserted between mm. 6 and 7, m. 8 would then be linked to m. 10. The result seems to be similar to the original passage in its overall meaning.

EXAMPLE 101.   Op. 82/IV, no. 3, mm. 4–11 (rearranged)

Such an experiment would corroborate Roman Brotbeck's analysis of Reger's *Clarinetten Quintett,* op. 146, in which he states, "With the reduction of the motifs to a few exchangeable elements, a mechanical and in a modern sense technical dimension influences the compositional process."[23]

Vier Sonatinen, op. 89 (1905, 1908)

The circumstances surrounding the composition of the *Vier Sonatinen*, op. 89, were quite similar to those determining the creation of the four collections of op. 82. As far as we know, the first two sonatinas were designed in 1905 without any external stimulus. The third and fourth sonatinas were composed in 1908 after the huge artistic and commercial success of the first two. As was the case with op. 82, the follow-up creations unfortunately did not measure up to the superb quality of the earlier works. Reger's purpose in writing these "second runs" was, of course, to take advantage of the previous successes, and to try to bolster not only his reputation, but also his financial position. After all, Reger was to a large extent dependent on the supplementary income provided by his concertizing and composing. He was also very conscious of his success as an artist and composer, and took advantage of any opportunity which in his eyes had the potential to strengthen his position in the music world.

The differences between the first two and the second two sonatinas are obvious with respect to genuine inventiveness, musical originality, and the composer's willingness and ability to submit to the formal principles of the sonata form. In all these areas the first two sonatinas are stronger and more convincing creations. For instance, the initial two themes or thematic groups in the 1905 sonatinas are distinct, well defined, and formally delineated with the same careful scrutiny a classical sonata by Mozart or the young Beethoven might show. The second two works are dominated more by Reger's tendency to manipulate his musical material irrespective of its intrinsic substance, which—despite his formidable constructive powers—seems to undermine the organic compositional process so obvious in particular in the *Sonatine e-moll,* op. 89, no. 1.

Many of Reger's contemporaries have testified that he could at any time unfailingly draw upon his immense craftsmanship. Regrettably, he sometimes got so entangled in this aspect of composition that the artistic, inspirational side of the creative process suffered considerably. The skilful and clever manipulation of musical ideas did not automatically result in valid artistic entities. It is unfortunate that Reger—probably as a consequence of the unceasing restlessness which permeated his whole life—did not always apply the same artistic scrutiny to his "musical children" as did his idol, Johannes Brahms.

Although Reger adheres to the classical sonata form in the first movements of all four sonatinas, the formal proportions in the last two are considerably less defined. The improvisatory elements are stronger, to the detriment of the formal concepts, and the phrase structure is more irregular in the later works. However, a certain "Mozartian" clarity is obvious in the transparent texture, in the frequent use of the *unisono* as a contrasting element, and in the classical formal and tonal schemes. This also holds for the two variation movements occurring in sonatinas no. 1 and no. 4, which clearly follow the model established by Mozart. In view of this general assessment, the first two sonatinas should be discussed in more detail.

Op. 89, no. 1 (E minor)

This work in three movements is by far the best of the four sonatinas and also the best known. It could be considered an initiation to the music of this composer for any young musician. The carefully balanced form of the first movement (*Allegro moderato e con espressione*), with its well defined characteristic theme groups, an effective development section dealing mostly with already established material, and a conventional recapitulation retaining the tonal schemes of the classical model—all this is combined with Reger's uncanny melodic and rhythmic inventiveness, that fuses these well defined musical concepts with his own harmonic language. The melodic and harmonic design of the first theme, with its Neapolitan progression at the end and its subsequent sequentation, is inimitably Regerian in style.

♪ *Continues on following page.*

EXAMPLE 102.   Op. 89, no. 1, mvt. 1, mm. 1–4

The second movement (*Andante con Variazioni*) contains a simple charming theme with four figurative variations, and follows the Mozartian variation model.

EXAMPLE 103.   Op. 89, no. 1, mvt. 2, mm. 1–5

In the last variation Reger uses his trademark, the "articulation group-ing," with convincing virtuosity. An intimate short *coda* concludes this charming movement—altogether a genuine musical gem.

Two distinct, contrasting themes constitute the basis for the last move-ment (*Vivace*), which is designed in a sonata-rondo form, since it lacks the usual repeats of the simple sonata form and uses new material for a kind of pseudo-development. The form is clearly A–B–A'–C–A–B–coda.

EXAMPLE 104.   Op. 89, no. 1, mvt. 3, mm. 1–6

The playful kaleidoscopic mastery of interlocking various figurative ele-ments so obvious in this sonatina elevates Reger to a position among the great masters of the past. This work not only provides superior teaching material, but is also an artistically unique and tremendously successful concert piece. Students generally respond with enthusiasm when assigned this piece.

Op. 89, no. 2 (D major)

The first movement (*Allegretto grazioso*) of this four-movement work is built on a rhythmically multifaceted first theme and a melodious second theme.

EXAMPLE 105A.   Op. 89, no. 2, mvt. 1, mm. 1–8

Op. 89, no. 2, mvt. 1, mm. 17–24

The thematic material is treated in a light, classical manner reminiscent of procedures which might be found in a sonatina by Clementi. The transparent texture also reflects the classical sonatina concept. Particularly characteristic is the modulatory development section (mm. 56 ff.), which simply states the various musical ideas in a skilful combinatory way, moving to rather distant keys (C sharp major in mm. 84 ff., for instance).

♪ *Continues on following page.*

The second movement (*Andantino*) is the only slow movement in op. 89 in A–B–A' song form. Its melodic lines seem to be determined by harmonic concepts rather than vice versa. The four-part writing in the repeated A' section relies heavily on chromatic passing tones, which Reger largely refrained from using in the first sonatina.

EXAMPLE 106A.   Op. 89, no. 2, mvt. 2, mm. 11–13 (A)

EXAMPLE 106B.   Op. 89, no. 2, mvt. 2, mm. 43–45 (A')

The third movement (*Vivace*) has all the ingredients of a scherzo with a
trio, although it is not designated as such. It is interesting to note that the
first four bars display the same rhythmical pattern in augmentation as the
first two bars of the slow movement. This resemblance certainly strength-
ens the overall unity of the work.

EXAMPLE 107A.   Op. 89, no. 2, mvt. 3, mm. 1–4

Also characteristic is the typical "insertion bar" (m. 8), which is the key element in this irregular nine-bar phrase. The "trio" is treated conventionally. Overall, Reger's focus seems to be on the intertwining of conventional harmonic progressions and *unisono* passages. The movement contains a number of quite charming and surprising harmonic effects, especially in mm. 32–35 and mm. 58–63.

EXAMPLE 108.   Op. 89, no. 2, mvt. 3, mm. 32–35

The fourth movement (*Allegro con spirito, ma non troppo vivace*) is designed in a loose sonata movement form and uses material typical of Reger's burlesque style. A very freely constructed middle section has development character. New and old materials are skilfully knitted together and contrasting figurations are imaginatively juxtaposed. However, Reger's occasional use of "ornamented" *unisono* passages, as in Example 109, might be considered by some a compositionally questionable effect.

EXAMPLE 109.   Op. 89, no. 2, mvt. 4, mm. 86–90

To the musically educated ear such a passage sounds somewhat strange. The question inevitably arises why Reger incorporated such a simplistic compositional device. Nevertheless, as teaching material this sonatina is certainly preferable to many run-of-the-mill "classical" sonatinas, such as some of Friedrich Kuhlau's, for example, since it is more diversified, harmonically interesting, and artistically of a good quality.

Sechs Präludien und Fugen, op. 99 (1906/07)

The value of this opus lies mainly in its instructive character, suitable in particular for composition students or anyone interested in the amalgamation of advanced harmonic concepts and a strict polyphonic style of writing. Romantic models of this genre do exist. Mendelssohn in particular composed some highly successful examples that also incorporate some pianistically interesting and appealing features. Max Reger, however, restricts himself to the models of the baroque period, in particular, of course, those by J.S. Bach. The compositional and inspirational quality varies considerably, even within single pieces. Interest is created mainly by imaginative combinations of motifs in several of the preludes (particularly no. 3), as well as by the skilful manipulation of the thematic material in some of the fugues (notably in no. 2). Some preludes follow figurative patterns similar to the *style brisé*, while others are contrapuntal or contain imitative writing. The fugues are all tonal—four in three voices, two in four voices. A few aspects may appear tedious, or at least not very imaginative, such as some of the figurative patterns in the preludes or a number of rather clumsily constructed polyphonic passages (for instance, in *Präludium* no. 4 and *Fuge* no. 5).

The best example for discussion is no. 6, with its intense melodic quality in the prelude and its intriguing double fugue.

Op. 99, no. 6 (D minor)

The prelude is a highly individualized utterance based on compositional acumen and intense musical expression. The *espressivo* element is enhanced through haunting chromaticisms embedded in varying densities of polyphonic writing. The combination of firm polyphonic elements with some improvisatory passages towards the end reflects well the basic idea of a prelude as it has evolved throughout music history. The last two bars leading to the *maggiore* in *pianissimo* reveal a unique harmonic structure and constitute a final cadence (*Schlußbildung*) characteristic of the mature Reger.

EXAMPLE 110.   Op. 99, no. 6, mm. 44–49

The fugue is based on a melodically well balanced diatonic first theme, complemented by a chromatic second theme.

EXAMPLE 111A.   Op. 99, no. 6, fugue, mm. 1–2 (first theme)

Reger adheres to well established patterns: separate expositions of both themes are followed by their appearance in double counterpoint, culminating in an exquisite climax with expanded sonorities, including the theme in the bass in octaves (mm. 56–58). This is a major accomplishment in the art of fugue writing, equal on a smaller scale to the mastery he displayed in the gigantic fugue of his *Bach Variations*, op. 81. As in that work, the strategically placed *marcato* signs at each theme entry indicate that Reger expects a strong dynamic and articulate emphasis.

LATE PERIOD

Towards the third period Reger concentrated increasingly on larger works with orchestra as the main focus of his compositional output. The few piano works from this period (opp. 115, 134, and 143), however, are exquisite masterworks reflecting an increasingly mature Regerian style of piano writing.

Max Reger caricature by
E. Burckhardt, 1907. (Max
Reger Institut)

Episoden, op. 115 (1910)

The subtitle of this collection of eight character pieces, *Klavierstücke für
große und kleine Leute*, might be somewhat misleading, since none of these
mature compositions can really be seen as suitable for "the little ones"
(*kleine Leute*). Schumann's *Kinderszenen*, op. 15, come to mind, which
were characterized by Schumann himself as "reflections of an older person." Reger's op. 115 should be seen in the same light. These pieces seem

to have been born out of a state of relaxation after the tremendous effort of the creation of another mountain peak of composition, the *Klavierkonzert*, op. 114. The psychological situation is similar to that in which *Aus meinem Tagebuch*, op. 82/I, was composed, as a respite immediately after the grandiose *Bach Variations*, op. 81. These follow-up works are of a much lighter musical character, less concentrated or intricate in textural and other compositional respects.

Like op. 82/I, this collection of pieces is on a rather high artistic level, although some pieces are weaker than others. No. 8, for example, abounds with rather superficial virtuosic figurations not counterbalanced by a healthy musical substance. In spite of these reservations one could imagine this set performed as a whole, if the sequence of the pieces were changed. The first five are all slow, introverted, and lyrical, while the last three belong to the category of vibrant rhythmically-oriented pieces in the usual Regerian burlesque style.

Still, it might be better to have a selection of three or four of the best pieces as a program point. One could think of nos. 6, 1, 3, and 7, or nos. 1, 4, and 7. The *Episoden* provide excellent teaching and performance material to acquaint the student with the mature Max Reger. Although most of the compositions are substantial enough to justify closer scrutiny, the selection of the four most poignant will suffice.

Op. 115, no. 1 (*Andante*)

This very poetic, lyrical gem in A–B–A'–coda form is characterized by extended lines and long phrases, which are not common in Reger's melodic thinking. The texture of inner broken harmonies is reminiscent of Schumann.

EXAMPLE 112.   Op. 115, no. 1, mm. 1–4

The leading melodic line is supported by extraordinary harmonic progressions of a highly expressionistic character, including some bold bi-tonal insinuations in mm. 32–34.

EXAMPLE 113.   Op. 115, no. 1, mm. 32–35

It would have been easy for Reger to soften the clashes between the pitches C and C sharp in m. 32 and between the pitches F and F sharp in m. 33 by altering the rhythmical structure of the melody. He could have interchanged the rhythmical design of the line on the second and fourth beats of these two 4/8 bars, writing eighth notes instead of sixteenth and vice versa. However, since he was determined not to avoid these strong *Querstände*, the performer should emphasize rather than conceal them. One is reminded here of one of Reger's most emphatic comments about the dissonance in his music in general, made in a letter to Emil Krause: "my music is not for those who are weak in the stomach . . . I prefer a ragout of dissonance."[24] Nevertheless, Reger incorporated with exquisite taste and refinement an extraordinary treatment of harmony within the context of a romantic character piece. (Note that there is a misprint in bar 13: the C sharp in the top contour should be an A, as in bar 49.)

Op. 115, no. 4 (*Andante sostenuto*)
Many of the textural formulas used here are reminiscent of Brahms, including the wide-spaced melodic arch in the beginning and the double third chain in mm. 19 ff. The very concise formal proportions provide for an architectural design that embraces a generous melodic flow and a continuously evolving elegiac expression. Important building elements are modulatory appendices which extend short phrases, as in mm. 2–3 and mm. 6–7.

EXAMPLE 114.   Op. 115, no. 4, mm. 1–7

These extensions are comparable to the typical Regerian interjection bars, which also appear in this piece in mm. 23–24.

EXAMPLE 115.   Op. 115, no. 4, mm. 23–24

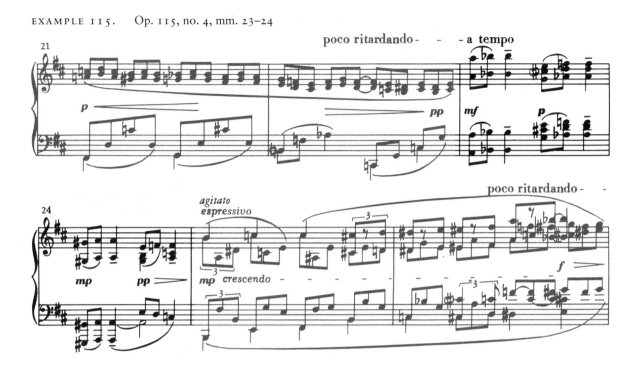

The aphoristic and sometimes declamatory character of the piece is caused by the juxtaposition of various motifs (see mm. 34–49). It is one of the best compositions in this collection and could be included in a concert program.

Op. 115, no. 5 (*Larghetto*)

The rather introspective mood based on and coloured by characteristic harmonies reveals the mature Reger now coming into his own. Pianistic formulas and corresponding sonorities are again stimulated by Brahms, Reger's inexhaustible source of inspiration. (Note especially the octave doublings and chords with thirds and sixths.)

EXAMPLE 116.   Op. 115, no. 5, mm. 1–6

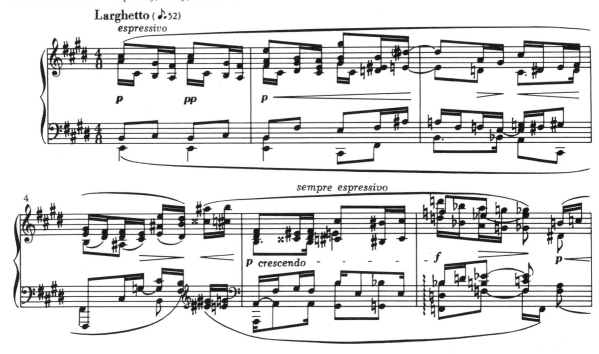

The phrase structure is less formal in organization and the harmonic progressions are much more expansive than in similar pieces by Brahms. The Procrustean bed of defined tonal centres has long been abandoned by Reger and replaced by a musical prose of endlessly flowing harmonic and melodic motion. The dense four-part *tessitura* enhances the harmonic intensity and contributes strongly to the expressive quality of this piece, which in combination with other suitable pieces could be a valuable addition to the repertoire of any advanced player.

Op. 115, no. 6 (*Vivace*)
Liszt's virtuosic style was obviously an inspiration for this brilliant concert piece, as seen in mm. 123–134.

EXAMPLE 117. Op. 115, no. 6, mm. 123–134

However, Reger has amalgamated such formulas quite idiosyncratically into his own style, which excels in original devices such as unison passages with passing notes (mm. 35–36 or 43–45), fast register changes (mm. 53–55), various characteristic broken chord patterns (mm. 99–101), and diatonic chordal progressions with passing notes (mm. 112–113).

EXAMPLE 118A. Op. 115, no. 6, mm. 35–36

Technically rather demanding, this *Episode* is certainly designed for the mature player (*große Leute*), as it requires agility and technical prowess as well as an extraordinary sensitivity to harmonic subtleties. The variety of challenging material makes it an excellent teaching piece for the advanced student.

Variationen und Fuge über ein Thema von G.Ph. Telemann, op. 134 (1914)

With the exception of the *Träume am Kamin*, op. 143, the *Telemann Variations* is the only major work for solo piano Max Reger composed during his Leipzig/Meiningen/Jena period. A comparison with the *Bach Variations*, op. 81, reveals the tremendous stylistic versatility of the composer. The style of the *Telemann Variations* is much less "romantic," less "philosophical," than that of op. 81. Of course, the thematic materials themselves could not be more contrasting.

EXAMPLE 119. Op. 134, mm. 1–8

Max Reger composing the *Ballet-Suite*, op. 130, in Kolberg, 1913. (Max Reger Institut)

The conventional proportions and the regular phrase structure of the theme—a minuet in the baroque binary form (:A:–:BA:) taken from Telemann's *Tafelmusik* in B flat major[25]—predetermine a totally different compositional approach than that inspired by the long, expanded melodic line from the Bach cantata used as a theme in op. 81. In addition, Reger's new idol, Mozart, and the transparency of his music motivate Reger's compositional processes, as previously demonstrated by the *Mozart Variations*, op. 132, for orchestra and their subsequent arrangement for two pianos, op. 132a. He seems determined now to follow the classical ideal of formal balance, regular phrase structure, and transparent texture, which in this case is also strongly influenced by technical and pianistic aspects. One could even consider this work a "compendium of Max Reger's pianistic style."[26]

The 23 variations are generally figurative and maintain the harmonic scheme of the theme and the formal proportions throughout. It is tempting to speculate whether Max Reger, who was so very susceptible to any artistic insinuation, might have seen a model in Brahms's *Handel Variations*. There are few common denominators that might support such a thesis. Aside from the concept of the variations and fugue as such, one could mention the choice of a formally very strict baroque theme and the tonality of the B flat major key signature, but that is where the similarities end. However, it is revealing that Reger himself, in a letter to his publisher, N. Simrock, writes that he can "say with good conscience that since Brahms's *Handel Variations* no such work has been created. . . . Op. 134 is without any doubt up to now my *best* piano work."[27]

Max Reger seemed to be more interested in designing pianistically challenging figurative variations than in creating emotionally balanced character variations as Brahms did. Since quite a number of the figurative patterns used are similar, the danger of repetitiveness can hardly be avoided (compare variations 5 and 22 in the following examples, or variations 6 and 19).

EXAMPLE 120A.   Op. 134, var. 5, mm. 1–2

EXAMPLE 120B.   Op. 134, var. 22, mm. 1–2

Only two variations use the typical polyphonic texture (nos. 10 and 16); all others are homophonic in design. Although one finds a number of slower, less virtuosic variations (nos. 10, 11, 15, 16, and 17) and a block of variations in the tonic minor key (nos. 16–18), one cannot escape the conclusion that they are placed more at random than strategically like those in op. 24 by Brahms, who exhibits an acute sixth sense for an amazingly harmonious balance, not only between the dramatic and lyrical, but also between the baroque and romantic elements.

The onslaught of the first nine brilliant, pianistically interesting, and technically challenging variations, all but two of which also adhere to the established dynamic scheme, *f–p–f*, could be perceived as oppressive, or at least tiring. Although superb and imaginative in themselves, in conjunction these various figurative formulas lack the necessary variety, which could have been achieved by the insertion of one or two more lyrical and relaxing variations. It is, of course, the responsibility of the performer to counteract the built-in danger of monotony by incorporating a maximum of dynamic diversification and expanding the possibilities of colouring to the utmost possible extreme.

The variations could be characterized as follows:

no. 1 and no. 2	melodic, figurative
no. 3 and no. 4	figurative, with chromaticism
no. 5 and no. 6	strong rhythmical figuration
no. 7	figurative, ethereal pianissimo scale patterns
no. 8 and no. 9	virtuosic pianistic patterns
no. 10	lyrical, slow, four-part writing
no. 11	lyrical with romantic melodious texture
no. 12 to no. 14	virtuosic figurative patterns
no. 15 to no. 17	slower, lyrical, closer to character variations
no. 18 to no. 22	virtuosic figurative patterns (no. 22 appearing as a double variation of no. 5)
no. 23	massive, organ-related sonorities

The introspective, rather mystical 8-bar bridge towards the beginning of the fugue is a most gratifying psychological preparation for the climax of contrapuntal writing that follows.

EXAMPLE 121.   Op. 134 (transition to the fugue)

Max Reger's artistic sensibility recognized the need for such a "musical prayer" linking the brilliant technical exuberance and carefree playfulness of the variations with the serene strictness of the following fugue. This unique and esoteric link constitutes a gravitational and psychological centre and is altogether one of the most moving passages in Reger's work.

The fugue was a form most meaningful to Reger, whose reverence for J.S. Bach's art in this genre was unlimited. It provided him with a perfect framework for his astounding ability to manipulate and combine themes and motifs contrapuntally. Within this form Reger often arrived at remarkable accomplishments, mainly for the organ, but also for solo piano (op. 81), for two pianos (op. 86, and op. 96), and for orchestra (op. 100 and op. 132). To intensify the climax, he often introduced a previous theme (either the theme of the variations or of a chorale) and combined it with the thematic material of the fugue as such. Although rather extended, the fugue in op. 134 does not contain this particular feature. On the surface it appears to be a double fugue with separate expositions of each theme and a subsequent combination of both. However the exposition of the second theme does not follow the strict rules of a self-contained exposition. Because of its rather subsidiary character one might even be tempted to call it an expanded contrapuntal motif.

The fugue contains a number of sections that are less strict polyphonically and oriented more towards a homophonic style, allowing the composer to introduce highly virtuosic figurations and thereby intensify the emphasis on pianistic aspects generally so prevalent in this work (see, for instance, mm. 60–94, or mm. 144–147 in the following example).

EXAMPLE 122. Op. 134, fugue, mm. 144–147

The thematic material is contrasting in nature. The main theme seems to be derived from the rhythmical exuberance of the original Telemann theme; the subsidiary second theme in its slow stepping motion has a more static character.

♪ *Continues on following page.*

EXAMPLE 123A.   Op. 134, fugue, mm. 1–7 (main theme)

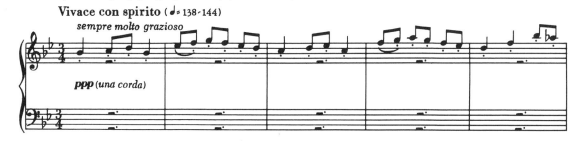

EXAMPLE 123B.   Op. 134, fugue, mm. 120-126 (subsidiary theme in the bass line)

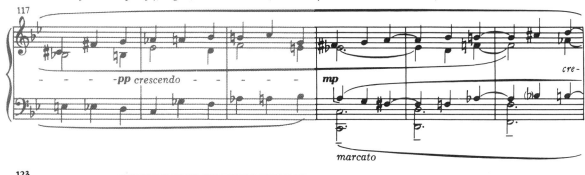

After the expositions Reger concentrates on the development of motifs taken mainly from the first theme. The compositional climax is reached at m. 200 through a combination of the first theme and the first six bars of the second theme in a dynamically and texturally massive setting.

EXAMPLE 124.   Op. 134, fugue, mm. 200–205

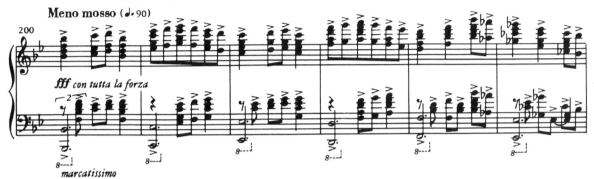

This flows into a finale of alternating chordal patterns brimming with a virtuosity reminiscent of Liszt. As in the fugue of op. 81, the performer is challenged to control the growth of dynamics in order to avoid over-extending the sound to oppressively extreme levels. In spite of Reger's extensive *fortissimo* indications, it is certainly advisable to "fall back" dynamically at certain strategic places in order to make room for a renewed dynamic growth.

Considering the textural complexities of his contrapuntal writing, the homophonic basis of the *Telemann Variations* testifies to Reger's joyful identification with an extremely virtuosic piano style. That and the conventional formal scheme derived from the theme, including the fairly predictable harmonic progressions in the fugue, make this "classical" work as accessible to the public as the more frequently performed *Mozart Variations*, op. 132, for orchestra.

However, only an excellent pianist should tackle this work. The performer requires not only superior technical stamina but also a keen sense of dynamic and agogic differentiation in order to present this work successfully on the concert stage without burning out the audience in a display of pyrotechnics.

Since heretical thoughts ought sometimes to be made public, if only for the sake of a fruitful discussion, one could argue that in a public performance of this piece it might be most effective to omit variations 6, 14, and 20, and possibly to place variation 19 between variations 16 and 17. The coherence of the work would be considerably strengthened.

Träume am Kamin, op. 143 (1915)

With this work, Reger created what is probably his most esoteric set of shorter pieces, in what he himself termed his "Free Jena Style" (see note 25, Chapter 2). A stringent economy of means is evident throughout. The composer, who has been searching all his life for the elusive balance of all the compositional elements constituting his musical language, seems now to have come close to that goal. From that point alone, his sudden death barely a year later was a tragedy, ending a turbulent artistic development just as it entered a definite stage of maturity.

His paramount focus is now on the essence of the musical idea, its most concentrated expression and elucidation, without any of the expanded dimensions or overloaded textures, sonorities, and dynamics that mark earlier works. The pieces are short. There is no longer the need to drive home a point. This new style is conducive to a concentrated expression in which every note has a meaningful place.

Most of the twelve pieces in op. 143 are introverted and lyrical, although a few are faster and lively, reflecting Reger's humorous buoyancy. Typically, all but one of the pieces end in *pp* or *ppp*, including the fast ones. One could see this as indicative of Reger's new attitude towards the character piece in general. In the area of solo piano music, he now probably considered this form as the chief avenue for expressing his deepest feelings and most intimate thoughts. The choice of the title, which can be translated as "Dreams by the Fireplace," clearly indicates that he must have considered the subconscious an important ingredient in the compositional process. This attitude is far removed from the deliberate displays of compositional prowess that often weakened rather than strengthened Reger's earlier compositions.

It is unfortunate that with op. 143, no. 12, Reger decided to include another metamorphosis of Chopin's *Berceuse*, as it seems out of place in this context. This "mirror image" could have some validity if one did not know the immortal model, but since the two pieces are so similar in concept and figuration, one can only regret that Reger found it necessary once more to tackle this old love of his and include it in this magnificent collection. If it was supposed to have been a reverence to the great master, this should have been noted. In contrast to the model, his concept is generally diatonic and down to earth, while Chopin's chromaticisms constitute the essence of an esoteric transcendence.

EXAMPLE 125.   Chopin, *Berceuse*, op. 57, mm. 45–46

*Continues on following page.*

Chopin was so much more successful in creating those glittering, magic cascades—a quality that eludes Reger, whose version sounds somewhat bland and ordinary.

EXAMPLE 126.　　Op. 143, no. 12, mm. 15–18

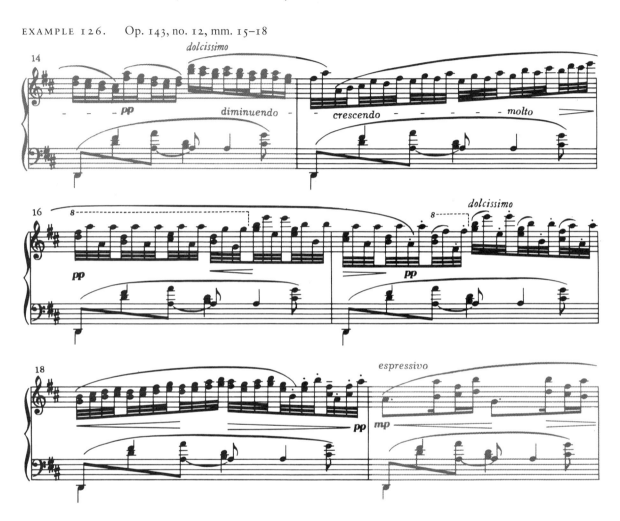

This cannot be considered more than a well worked out experiment crudely imitating Chopin's style. Unlike all the other pieces in this collection, it is not a valid artistic statement in its own right.

In view of the consistent quality of all the other pieces, it is difficult to select a few for closer scrutiny. The following choice is arbitrary, and based on personal preference.

Op. 143, no. 2 (*Con moto*)

At first sight this piece might be considered a derivative imitation of Brahms.

EXAMPLE 127.   Op. 143, no. 2, mm. 1–6

However, with due recognition of the many stylistic elements which can be traced to this composer, one also has to acknowledge the total transformation of these elements into Reger's own inimitable expression. Admittedly, the model is perceptible, but the Regerian harmonic concepts and modulatory boldness far transcend it. Reger arrives at something new. This process is comparable to Beethoven's use of Haydn's procedures in sonata writing, transforming them into his own.

Max Reger's step backward into the simplicity of melodic, harmonic, and textural designs was actually a step forward towards the formalization of his own mature language. As in Schubert's music, tiny harmonic shifts take on a powerful and essential quality within the simplified context.

EXAMPLE 128.   Op. 143, no. 2, mm. 33–38

In performance one should trace the harmonic subtleties and create an awareness of their emotional weight within the overall context. Attention to exquisitely differentiated dynamics and the use of considerable agogic freedom will help to shape the interlocking phrases with a maximum of expressiveness.

Op. 143, no. 4 (*Allegretto grazioso*)

This unassuming, charming *gavotte* is written with a textural austerity unusual even for the mature Reger.

EXAMPLE 129.   Op. 143, no. 4, mm. 1–7

Strongly articulated staccato passages contrast with a legato middle section (*andante*), in which the congruence of the differentiated dynamic indications and the subtle harmonic shifts are essential features of the music and should be closely observed in the interpretation. The usual irregular phrase structure should not interfere with an intuitive perception of a formal coherence. The sometimes ascetic use of sonorities, so uncharacteristic of Reger, is fitting and witty, and leads to an unusual concentration of the musical substance.

♪ *Continues on following page.*

EXAMPLE 130. Op. 143, no. 4, mm. 17–22

As far as the interpretation is concerned, it seems important to apply a technical approach that allows the fingers to dance off rather than stitch into the keys, thus achieving the expected feather-light elasticity.

Op. 143, no. 6 (*Poco vivace*)
Although this piece seems to be a study along the lines of figurative models provided by Chopin, its chromaticisms combined with a tremendous variety in motion and rising and falling contours create a nearly impressionistic effect, evoking the shimmer of thousands of lights reflected from rippling water. With the passing notes always congruent with the harmonic rhythm, the wavelike shape of the line is juxtaposed against a firm rhythmical structure.

EXAMPLE 131. Op. 143, no. 6, mm. 1–10

This, for Reger, rather unusual piece reveals again his seemingly unlimited power of imagination. It begins with a "prefix" of two bars, a concept
comparable to the interjection bars frequently found in his music. Pianistic
flexibility and technical agility are as necessary for the realization of this
piece as for the equivalent figurative patterns of Chopin's F minor *Étude*,
op. 25, no. 2.

♪ *Continues on following page.*

Op. 143, no. 8 (*Vivace*)

As a matter of curiosity, this "White Key Etude" is mentioned as a counter-part to Chopin's "Black Key Etude," op. 10, no. 5. Although not of a similar artistic quality, it is an interesting realization of the envisaged concept. The restriction of the figurative aspect to three basic components (see Example 132) results in a certain superficiality, which can be counteracted by playing the piece as fast as possible (fulfilling the request implied by Reger's metronome indication of 160 per quarter note).

EXAMPLE 132A.   Op. 143, no. 8, mm. 1–5

EXAMPLE 132B.   Op. 143, no. 8, mm. 11–15

EXAMPLE 132C.   Op. 143, no. 8, mm. 26–30

Op. 143, no. 10 (*Vivace*)

As a wonderful example of Reger's boisterous burlesque style, this
humoreske is perhaps the most focused and concentrated specimen found
in his whole oeuvre for piano.

EXAMPLE 133. Op. 143, no. 10, mm. 1–8

This piece is formally as concise as one can imagine (even the short contrasting middle section is integrated rather than set off from the main section). The continuity is never interrupted, in spite of the many contrasting
figurative elements used. The *un poco meno* towards the end is one of the
most imaginative codas Reger ever wrote.

♪ *Continues on following page.*

EXAMPLE 134. Op. 143, no. 10, mm. 124–133

Most musicians familiar with Max Reger's work would probably agree that this exquisitely brilliant concert piece should appear more often in piano recital programs. It shows Max Reger at his best in a genre which he virtually created.

WORKS WITHOUT OPUS NUMBERS

In addition to those works discussed so far, quite a number of single pieces and a few collections did not receive opus numbers for one reason or another. Most of these pieces are either earlier works, like the *Sechs Klavierstücke, Grüße an die Jugend* (1898), or occasional compositions such as the *Fughette über das Deutschlandlied* (1916) or curiosities such as the *Marsch der Stiftsdamen* (1914) that do not deserve particular attention. However, one should mention the didactic collection of 111 two- and three-part *Kanons* (1895) as a compendium of Max Reger's contrapuntal mastery and the short but extremely well crafted *Vier Spezialstudien für die linke Hand* (1901) as a welcome addition to that particular genre.

The *Blätter und Blüten* (1898–1902), a collection of short ordinary genre pieces composed on various occasions, cannot compare in quality with collections such as op. 44. Most of the pieces are uninspiring or trite and are generally mixtures of various stylistic influences. The only piece in which Reger seems to anticipate his later musical self is the *Elegie*, no. 4, which shows some harmonically intriguing and densely chromatic passages.

EXAMPLE 135.   *Elegie*, no. 4, mm. 19–20

The metric indicator is 6/16, a pulsation which is in constant friction with the 3/8 figurations of the melodic line. This ambivalence must be part of the interpretive process. It is not easy, but is nevertheless possible, to insinuate this type of rhythmic fluctuation by emphasizing two beats per bar.

More substantial are the *Fünf Spezialstudien nach Chopin* (1899), which are arrangements for piano of three waltzes (op. 64, nos. 1 and 2, and op. 42), the *Etude*, op. 25, no. 6, and the *Impromptu*, op. 29. The substantial number of arrangements attests to Reger's admirable skills in this genre. In this particular case, the arrangement procedure consists mainly of intensifying the texture through added figuration or filling in parallel lines, similar to the technique Godowsky used for some of his famous arrangements, which are as a whole more imaginative and pianistically more rewarding.

It is not quite clear whether the term *Studien* (which Hans Pfitzner also uses for his op. 51) refers more to compositional aspects or to the technical side of pianism. The comment on fingering that Reger included seems to point to the latter. He indicates that the advanced player might perform these pieces in public and leaves the choice of the fingering to him or her, assuming that the pianist who might tackle these pieces would be advanced enough to know the principles of fingering. He also does not want to infringe on the artistic freedom of the player, although he recommends practising the studies in legato as well as staccato.[28]

The artistic value of these pieces is rather limited and the inherent elegance of Chopin's music suffers considerably, as can be seen in the following examples showing excerpts from Reger's arrangement and Chopin's original *Impromptu*, op. 29.

EXAMPLE 136A.   *Impromptu*, mm. 1–4, by Reger

EXAMPLE 136B.   *Impromptu*, op. 29, mm. 1–4, by Chopin

The most valuable collection of works without opus numbers is the *Vier Klavierstücke*, op. posthumous (1901–1906). The four pieces are entitled *Improvisation* (no. 1), *Perpetuum mobile* (no. 2), *Nachtstück* (no. 3), and *Romanze* (no. 4). Although they are substantial, they cannot be considered a set, since they were composed over a period of several years and show no discernible compositional or emotional similarities or motivic interrelationships. Three fall into the category of the sonorous "Brahmsian chordal style," incorporating complex romantic textures reminiscent of Reger's greatest idol, and including some stark rhythmic devices that add impact and drama, in particular to nos. 1 and 3. The most characteristic piece of the collection is probably no. 1.

♪ *Continues on following page.*

Improvisation, no. 1 (*Sehr schnell und aufgeregt*)

Rhythm and texture in this "very fast and excited" piece are similar to those of the relevant stylistic model by Brahms, op. 116, no. 1 (see Example 67) or his own prototype, op. 79a, no. 3 (Example 68).

EXAMPLE 137. *Improvisation*, no. 1, mm. 1–9

The dominance of harmony as the decisive structural element is obvious. The melodic aspect is reduced to splinters totally dependent on and determined by the ever-changing, vacillating harmonies. Even the more coherent melodic line in the short contrasting middle section has the character of an aphorism rather than a substantial melodic statement.

However, the purely pianistic aspects are genuine and quite effectively deployed within the syncopated, chordal structure. The massive harmonically quickly changing and fast-moving sound patterns are rhythmically enlivened by the frequent use of the *hemiola*, which may account for the perceived affinity to the dramatic *melos* of Brahms.

EXAMPLE 138. *Improvisation*, no. 1, mm. 78–81

A mature virtuosity is essential to master this piece, which could be included in any concert program within a carefully weighted selection of three or four other pieces by Max Reger.

OTHER MUSIC FOR PIANO

Although not strictly within the bounds of this discussion of Max Reger's music for solo piano, the substantial *Klavierkonzert*, op. 114 (1910), as well as some of the important works for piano duet and two pianos should at least be mentioned. The latter in particular played an important role in Reger's concertising. The profound *Variationen und Fuge über ein Thema von Ludwig van Beethoven*, op. 86 (1904), was a mainstay in Reger's own concert programs. In addition, the massive *Introduktion, Passacaglia, und Fuge*, op. 96 (1906), was often performed by Reger with various pianists. His most frequent duo partners were August Schmid-Lindner, Willi Jinkertz, Philipp Wolfrum, and Henriette Schelle. Reger's contribution to the piano duet literature includes six collections of pieces, the most notable being the *Cinq Pièces Pittoresques*, op. 34 (1899), the *Sechs Burlesken*, op. 58 (1901), and the *Sechs Stücke*, op. 94 (1906). These compositions constitute a substantial contribution to the rather limited repertoire for piano duet and could be a meaningful portion of the teaching repertoire for more advanced piano students.

5

THE INTERPRETIVE FACTOR

It is a truism that every composer wants his or her music to reach a sympathetic audience and to be performed by congenial interpreters. But Max Reger's concern in this regard seems to have been more deeply rooted, as is revealed in his various comments to the effect that he felt the urgent necessity to establish a "tradition"[1] for the interpretation of his music. He must have feared that the accepted romantic performance practice of his time was not satisfactory for this new type of musical utterance that caused so much controversy, especially during his "Munich Period." Yet he might also have been consciously or subconsciously aware of particular qualities of performance practice that formed a constituent part of the compositional process, and which only he as the composer could provide.

The available information consists mainly of reports describing Max Reger's own piano playing, his pianistic idiosyncrasies, and his relationship to sound production and to the preferred piano sound in general. In addition, there are a few recordings of interpretations by Max Reger himself taken from the Welte-Mignon System (see note 11, Chapter 4).

The most important Regerian characteristic that emerges from such information is what could be called a creative flexibility, pertaining to most if not all aspects of the performance process, including tempo, rhythmic

Max Reger, 1908. Photograph by R. Dührkoop. (Max Reger Institut)

pulse, dynamics, phrasing, articulation, agogic accentuation, vertical sound differentiation, and more. Although Max Reger was adamant that his profuse expression markings (written in red ink in his autographs) should be meticulously followed, he was certainly prone to succumbing in a performance situation to the inspiration of the moment and changing preconceived procedures on the spot. This was typical of the romantic performance practice in general, although it seemed to have been especially pronounced in Reger's own playing. It was also an outlet for the performing composer, who can, of course, change details of an established composition or even improvise certain variants in the moment of performance. This type of artistic freedom has largely disappeared today. The modern "legitimacy" of objectivity and style, based on historical research and excellent *urtext* editions, leaves little room to manoeuvre, unless one chooses to contest the established schools of interpretation for the sake of challenge, as did the indefatigable Glenn Gould.

Anyone performing Max Reger's piano music today might render a distinct disservice to the composer with the modern, *urtext*-oriented approach, which more often than not amounts to an acoustic X-ray of black signs on white paper. Without a particular romantic awareness of the many expressive possibilities that must be allowed to evolve from the music intuitively, without premeditation, a performer is very likely to fail to come close to Reger's intentions. Although composers might not always be the best interpreters of their own works, even some of their weaker efforts usually provide clear indications of their artistic intentions. In spite of the pianistic insufficiencies in Ravel's own interpretation of his *Sonatina*, for instance, one can clearly perceive the underlying musical ideas, perhaps even better than in an uninspired, over-produced modern recording.

In the few recordings available of Max Reger's playing, his pianistic expertise and imaginative approach are readily discernible. Reger's recording of the *Humoreske*, op. 20, no. 5 (see note 11, Chapter 4), in particular abounds in examples of his feather-light touch, ingenious pedal effects, ample rhythmic freedom, exquisite phrasing, and many other expressive qualities. It would be highly desirable for today's pianists to transfer this type of approach to their own interpretations of Reger's piano music. As indicated by Reger's markings in the orchestral scores he was preparing for the concerts of the Meininger Hofkapelle, he was extremely concerned about the realization of an exquisitely differentiated sound spectrum as the carrier of the musical idea. The annotations were sometimes excessive, certainly by modern standards, but again, they are indicative of the specific understanding Max Reger had about music in general and his own music in particular. One can safely assume that the composition as such was only the *status nascendi,* leading via the interpretation to the true reality of the work. It might thus be helpful to establish a few characteristic performance guidelines derived from the available information.

With respect to tempo as such and the continuation and alteration of tempo within a given context, it is obvious that Reger expected a maximum of freedom, far beyond our modern sometimes ascetic and stereotypical performance practice. His own choice of tempi was very much influenced by the inspiration of the moment.[2] His metronome markings are to be taken with a grain of salt and considered a maximum (see note 19, Chapter 4). Max Reger's declared aim was "clarity." The tempo has to be slow enough to allow the listener to follow the harmonic intricacies and textural complexities of the music. Should these two characteristics increase—which usually happens towards climaxes—the tempo should automatically be modified, following the built-in expansion, and thus slow down. The reverse is possible, although not as frequent. The continuum of a given pulse is also determined by the phrase structure: it is flexible to a large degree, usually increasing slightly towards the apex of a phrase and relaxing towards the end. One might say that this is nothing new in the art of romantic interpretation. However, in Reger's music it is a question of degree, and—commensurate with the general characteristics of his personality—the relevant spectrum is extremely wide. For example, Max Reger was known to shade his *pianissimo* to such an extent that some people complained it was inaudible.

Exquisite dynamic shading is a major portion of Reger's complex phrase structure. His own phrasing in performances was praised as extremely natural. In addition, he reportedly emphasized what were for him the most important parts and to a large extent subdued other voices, however interesting they might be.[3] Although the composer generally counteracts the possible monotony of repetitious two-bar phrases by increasing the figuration in subsequent appearances, additional dynamic diversification far beyond the indications written in the score is necessary in support of this process. It is essential to comprehend the larger, encompassing "superphrases" without which Max Reger's music would be unbearably disjointed. The transformation of such insight into the reality of sound requires intelligence and an extraordinary sensitivity on the part of the performer.

Contrasts in articulation in general cannot be overemphasized. In particular, the stroke signs (wedges) and staccato dots should be distinguished as clearly as possible and set off distinctly from any groupings of notes under a slur or phrasing line. The rhythmical elasticity expected requires mental alertness and very agile physical movements and strokes.

The most difficult task in the interpretation of Reger's music is to create an elucidating transparency for his often overloaded texture. Reger was reportedly able in his own playing to emphasize boldly one particularly important facet and relegate the rest to the background. He seemed obsessed with thematic material and its contrapuntal relevance—hence the many *marcato* signs in his fugues whenever the theme appears. This technique of a kind of chiaroscuro polyphony was the basis of a permanent oscillation stimulated by the musical necessities in every moment.

A very important aspect of interpretation, frequently referred to by Reger's critics and friends, is the way he applied agogic accents to clarify his bold harmonic progressions. Critics sometimes even chastised other performers in Reger's time for not achieving the same intoxicating sound and agogic expressiveness that he did.[4]

In his early chamber music Max Reger used a special sign (𝆒) over certain notes and even rests in order to emphasize particular rhythmical and harmonic points within the musical structure.

EXAMPLE 139.   Op. 1, *Finale*, mm. 121–124

EXAMPLE 140. Op. 3, mvt. 3, mm. 59–61

Max Reger did not continue the application of this sign. It seems that he replaced it by the *tenuto* sign ($\bar{\rho}$), which he uses frequently. It is safe to assume that the *tenuto* sign in Reger's music has stronger agogic implications than normally expected, since it is frequently used to emphasize syncopations, as in mm. 2 and 3 of the third *Humoreske*, op. 20.

EXAMPLE 141.   *Humoreske*, op. 20, no. 3, mm. 1–6

Andante grazioso

leggiero e sempre grazioso

In view of the complex harmonic language with its constantly shifting tonal centres, it seems reasonable to expect any performer to underline important harmonic progressions by a commensurate agogic emphasis. The marked example below, taken from the *Sonate für Violine und Klavier*, op. 72, can be considered exemplary in this respect. For instance, in order to understand the harmony, a considerable rubato is necessary in bars 136–137 and 140.

♪ *Continues on following page.*

EXAMPLE 142.   Op. 72, mvt. I, mm. 126–144

It was the unanimous opinion of all who heard Reger perform that his singing legato combined with a most exquisite sound was one of the most fascinating characteristics of his playing style. The important Berlin critic Paul Bekker recommended that "all who want to come closer to Reger's piano music should study this kind of interpretation . . . based predominantly on the technique of legato playing."[5]

In this context it is essential for the modern Reger interpreter to cultivate to the extreme the ability to shade inner voices according to their harmonically functional values. This is particularly important in the many passages containing the characteristic organ-style chord progressions.

EXAMPLE 143.   *Telemann Variations, Op. 134, var. 16, mm. 25–28*

The use of the pedal in Reger's piano music has a particular interpretive meaning which goes beyond the usual functional application. Like that of any romantic composer, his sound spectrum is based on the continuous and, of course, differentiated use of the pedal. However, the particular idiosyncrasy of a smooth shifting and gliding from one harmony into the next often requires a sophisticated use of the half pedal.

This effect is particularly obvious in the few available recordings of Reger performing his own piano music. In addition, there are reports that Reger often used too much pedal even by the standards of the day, especially in the interpretation of Bach and Mozart. It is also apparent that Reger preferred very softly voiced instruments, like the Ibach and Blüthner grand pianos, which he found ideal for accompaniments. In a letter to Philipp Wolfrum he emphasized, "I am only playing Ibach; the factory is producing extraordinarily beautiful grand pianos. . . ."[6] These instruments had sound characteristics different from those our modern instruments are

Programme of an all-Reger chamber music concert with the composer participating as a pianist, 1907. (Max Reger Institut)

Städtischer Musik~Verein
Düsseldorf.

Montag, den 25. Februar 1907,

abends 7 Uhr,

im Kaisersaale der Städtischen Tonhalle:

II. Kammermusik - Abend

Reger-Abend.

1. **Suite** in altem Stil, F-dur op. 93, für Violine und Pianoforte,
   Präludium (Allegro commodo, non troppo vivace)
   Largo — Fuge.
   Herr Konzertmeister Jul. Röntgen und der Komponist.

2. **Fünf Lieder**
   gesungen von Frau Anna Erler-Schnaudt aus München.
   Am Klavier der Komponist.

3. **Serenade** für Flöte, Violine u. Viola, D-dur op. 77a,
   Allegro. Andante semplice con variazioni. Presto.
   Herr R. Pocteinzky, Herr Konzertmeister J. Röntgen
   und Herr H. Köhler.

4. **Fünf Lieder**
   Frau Anna Erler-Schnaudt und der Komponist.

5. **Introduktion, Passacaglia und Fuge**
   für zwei Pianoforte, op. 96.
   Frau Henriette Schelle aus Cöln und der Komponist.

Die beiden Konzertflügel sind von der Firma Rudolf Ibach,

Düsseldorf, Schadowstrasse 52.

Programm 20 Pfg.

designed to yield. They provided a mellowness of sound and allowed for a roundness of contour far removed from our modern ideal of aggressive and sometimes merciless percussive sonorities.

One should not forget that Reger in his time could have been considered a musical representative of expressionism comparable to some of the German expressionist painters, like Heckel, Kirchner, Macke, or Nolde. (As a point of interest, it should be mentioned that one of the most striking and powerful portraits of Max Reger was painted by the German expressionist Max Beckmann). It seems to puzzle musicologists that the Schoenberg circle in Vienna was quite fond of his music. However, this is not at all unusual, since the very expansion of tonal procedures in Reger's music fell well within the initial ideas and aims of the Second Viennese School. Tone colour in general played an ever increasing role as an important vehicle in the transmission of musical ideas—hence the trend away from the piano towards the orchestra or various new and unusual combinations of instruments.

It seems therefore paramount not to underestimate the important role the sustaining pedal plays in Reger's piano music as an essential means of colouring and intensifying his expansive harmonic concepts. In Reger's original scores only a few specific pedal markings can be found. In some cases the pedal indications are those of editors (note, for instance, op. 44, Universal Edition). However, indications like *sempre con pedale*, sometimes cautiously modified by additional attributes like *ma delicato*, do appear. The best and most instructive examples are found in the *Bach Variations*, op. 81. Some of them can only be seen as very generous. The composer must have had colour in mind, since the effects are sometimes rather impressionistic, as in the following example:

EXAMPLE 144.   *Bach Variations*, op. 81, m. 48

Finally, Max Reger seems to expect from the interpreter the strongest possible identification with the musical content and meaning. Like learning a language the syntax of which is only superficially familiar, the study of Max Reger's music requires intense attention and love, without which it will elude one's understanding and remain forever an enigma. Those, however, who have been grasped by the special spiritual power inherent in all great music might have the same inner visions upon hearing Reger's music that the poet Hermann Hesse in his essay "Eine Sonate" so beautifully ascribes to Hedwig Dillenius, who is enraptured by this music played for her by her brother Ludwig, while her husband finds it simply "too original." "It is a matter of taste," he says, and returns to his daily routine. It seems that in a few pages, Hesse not only catches the essence of Reger's music, but also instinctively characterizes the two opposing camps that always existed and probably always will be present as long as Reger's music is performed.

> Ludwig played, and she saw a dark expanse of water move in high rhythmic waves. A flock of immense, powerful birds approached with thundering wingbeats, in primordial gloom. The storm drummed on, and now and then threw foaming crests up into the air, where they shattered in a shower of tiny pearls. Through the roar of the waves, the wind, and the great wingbeat, something mysterious resounded—a song, sung now with heavy pathos, now with the delicate voice of a child—an intimate, lovely melody.
>
> Clouds fluttered black in ragged strands, through which opened wondrous glimpses of the deep golden heavens beyond. Hideous sea monsters rode the great breakers, while chubby cherubs with the eyes of little children circled playfully, delicately over the smaller waves. And terror was overcome by the growing magic of loveliness, and the scene was transformed into a light, airy world between worlds from which all weight had been lifted. Delicate elfin creatures danced in rings, suspended in the moon-like light, and sang ethereal, effortlessly floating melodies with incorporeal voices pure as crystal.
>
> But then it seemed as if it were no longer the angelic elves themselves who sang, hovering in the glowing whiteness, but rather the person who

told or dreamt of them. A heavy drop of yearning and unsoothable human suffering fell into this radiant world of contented beauty, and in place of paradise there stood a human dream of paradise—no less dazzling, but its beauty accompanied by the deep resonance of an unstillable longing for home.[7]

MAX REGER IN A
SYNCRON-OPTIC VIEW

		1890	Op. 1—Sonata, violin and piano
		1891	Op. 2—Trio, violin, viola and piano
			Op. 3—Sonata, violin and piano
1892	Op. 9—12 Walzer-Capricen (duet)	1892	Op. 5—Sonata, cello and piano
1893	Op. 10—Deutsche Tänze (duet)		
1894	Op. 11—7 Walzer		
	Op. 13—Lose Blätter, 14 kleine Klavierstücke		
1895	Op. 17—Aus der Jugendzeit, 20 kleine Klavierstücke		
1896	Op. 18—Improvisationen, 8 Klavierstücke		
1897	Op. 20—5 Humoresken		
1898	Op. 22—6 Walzer (duet)	1898	Op. 28—Sonata, violin and piano
	Op. 24—Six Morceaux		
	Op. 25—Aquarellen		
	Op. 26—7 Fantasiestücke		
1899	Op. 32—7 Charakterstücke	1899	Op. 41—Sonata, violin and piano
	Op. 36—Bunte Blätter, 9 kleine Stücke		
1900	Op. 44—10 kleine Vortragsstücke	1900	Op. 49—2 Sonatas, clarinet and piano
	Op. 45—6 Intermezzi		
	Op. 53—Silhouetten, 7 Stücke		
1901	Op. 58—6 Burlesken (duet)		
	Op. 79a—10 Kompositionen		
		1902	Op. 64—Piano Quintet
1903	Op. 81—Bach-Variationen	1903	Op. 72—Sonata, violin and piano
	Op. 82/1—Aus meinem Tagebuch I		
1904	Op. 86—Beethoven-Variationen (2 pianos)	1904	Op. 78—Sonata, cello and piano
	Op. 89/1—Sonatine e-moll		Op. 79d—Wiegenlied, Cappricio, Burla, violin and piano
	Op. 89/2—Sonatine D-dur		Op. 79e—Caprice, Kleine Romanze, cello and piano
1905	Op. 82/2—Aus meinem Tagebuch	1905	Op. 84—Sonata, violin and piano
	Op. 94—6 Stücke (duet)		Op. 87—Albumblatt, Romanze, violin and piano
	Op. 96—Introduktion, Passacaglia und Fuge (2 pianos)		
1906	Op. 99—6 Präludien und Fugen	1906	Op. 93—Suite im alten Stil, violin and piano
1907	Op. 89/3—Sonatine F-dur		
	Op. 89/4—Sonatine a-moll		
1908	Op. 114—Klavierkonzert mit Orchester	1908	Op. 102—Trio, violin, cello and piano
	Op. 115—Episoden, 8 Klavierstücke		Op. 103a—Suite, violin and piano
1909	Op. 82/3—Aus meinem Tagebuch	1909	Op. 103b—2 Little Sonatas, violin and piano
			Op. 107—Sonata, clarinet and piano
1910	Op. 82/4—Aus meinem Tagebuch	1910	Op. 113—Piano Quartet
			Op. 116—Sonata, cello and piano
		1911	Op. 122—Sonata, violin and piano
1912	Op. 132a—Mozart-Variationen (2 pianos)		
1913	Op. 134—Telemann-Variationen		
1914	Op. 143—Träume am Kamin, 12 kleine Klavierstücke	1914	Op. 133—Piano Quartet
		1915	Op. 139—Sonata, violin and piano
		1916	Op. 103c—12 kleine Stücke nach eigenen Liedern, violin and piano

IMPORTANT OTHER WORKS	HISTORICAL CONTEXT
	1889 *R. Strauss—Don Juan*
	1890 Early Period: Wiesbaden (studies with Hugo Riemann)
	1893 *J. Brahms—Klavierstücke Op. 116–119*
	1894 *C. Debussy—Prélude à l'après-midi d'un faune*
1898 Op. 27—Chorale Fantasia 'Ein' feste Burg ist unser Gott' (Organ)	1898 Moves back to family in Weiden
	1899 *A. Schoenberg—Verklärte Nacht*
1900 Op. 46—Fantasia and Fugue on B–A–C–H (Organ) Op. 54—String Quartets	
	1901 Middle Period: Munich *S. Rachmaninoff—Second Piano Concerto*
1903 Op. 73—Variations and Fugue on an Original Theme (Organ)	1902 Marriage to Elsa von Bercken
1903–12 Op. 76—Schlichte Weisen (Voice and Piano)	
1905 Op. 90—Sinfonietta (Orchestra)	
1906 Op. 95—Serenade (Orchestra)	
1907 Op. 100—Variations and Fugue on a Theme of J.A. Hiller (Orchestra)	1907 Late Period: Universtätsmusikdirektor in Leipzig
1908 Op. 101—Violin Concerto	1908 *B. Bartók—First String Quartet*
	1909 *A. Schoenberg—Three Piano Pieces Op. 11*
1910 Op. 118—String Sextet	
	1911 Hofkapellmeister in Meiningen
1912 Op. 124—"An die Hoffnung" (Contralto and Orchestra)	
1913 Op. 128—4 Tondichtungen nach Arnold Böcklin (Orchestra)	1913 *I. Stravinsky—Le Sacre du printemps*
1914 Op. 132—Variations and Fugue on a Theme of Mozart (Orchestra)	1914 Lives in Jena
1915 Op. 131c—3 Suites for Cello solo Op. 146—Quintet for Clarinet and Strings	

WORKS FOR SOLO PIANO

Identified below the opus number and title of each work are the date and publisher of the first edition, followed by the present publisher(s), based on information from the Breitkopf & Härtel Gesamtausgabe.

op. 11   *Sieben Walzer*
        (1894, Augener; Schott)

op. 13   *Lose Blätter, 14 kleine Klavierstücke*
        (1894, Augener; Schott)

op. 17   *Aus der Jugendzeit, 20 kleine Klavierstücke*
        (1902, Augener; Schott)

op. 18   *Improvisationen, 8 Klavierstücke*
        (1902, Augener; Schott)

op. 20   *Fünf Humoresken*
        (1899, Joseph Aibl Verlag; Universal Edition)

op. 24   *Six Morceaux pour le Piano*
        (1899, Robert Forberg; Peters)

op. 25   *Aquarelle, kleine Tonbilder*
        (1902, Augener; Schott)

op. 26   *Sieben Fantasiestücke*
        (1899, Robert Forberg; Peters)

op. 32   *Sieben Charakterstücke*
          (1899, Joseph Aibl Verlag; Universal Edition)

op. 36   *Bunte Blätter, 9 kleine Stücke*
          (1899, Joseph Aibl Verlag; Universal Edition)

op. 44   *Zehn kleine Vortragsstücke zum Gebrauch beim Unterricht*
          (1900, Joseph Aibl Verlag; Universal Edition, Henle)

op. 45   *Sechs Intermezzi*
          (1900, Joseph Aibl Verlag; Universal Edition)

op. 53   *Silhouetten, 7 Stücke*
          (1901, Joseph Aibl Verlag; Universal Edition)

op. 79a   *Zehn Klavierstücke*
          (1903–08, Hermann Beyer & Söhne, Sikorski)

op. 81   *Variationen und Fuge über ein Thema von J.S. Bach*
          (1904, Lauterbach & Kuhn; Bote & Bock, Universal Edition)

op. 82   *Aus meinem Tagebuch*
          vol. I:(1904, Lauterbach & Kuhn; Bote & Bock, Universal Edition)
          vol. II: (1906, Lauterbach & Kuhn; Bote & Bock, Universal Edition)
          vol. III: (1911, Bote & Bock, Universal Edition)
          vol. IV:(1912, Bote & Bock, Universal Edition)

op. 89   *Vier Sonatinen*
          nos. 1 and 2: (1905, Lauterbach & Kuhn; Bote & Bock, Universal Edition)
          nos. 3 and 4: (1908, Lauterbach & Kuhn; Bote & Bock, Universal Edition)
          Complete edition: (Peters, Henle)

op. 99   *Sechs Präludien und Fugen*
          (1907, Lauterbach & Kuhn; Bote & Bock, Universal Edition)

op. 115   *Episoden, Klavierstücke für große und kleine Leute*
          (1910, Bote & Bock, Universal Edition)

op. 134   *Variationen und Fuge über ein Thema von G.Ph. Telemann*
          (1914, Simrock; Peters)

op. 143   *Träume am Kamin, 12 kleine Klavierstücke*
          (1916, Simrock; Peters)

All the works above are also available within the Breitkopf & Härtel Gesamtausgabe.

The following works are without opus numbers.

Präludium und Fuge g-moll
(1986, Breitkopf & Härtel Gesamtausgabe, vol. 38)

Grande Valse de Concert
(1986, Breitkopf & Härtel Gesamtausgabe, vol. 38)

111 Kanons durch alle Dur- und Molltonarten
(1895, Augener; Schott)

Etude Brillante (originally part of op. 18)
(1910, Schott; Breitkopf & Härtel Gesamtausgabe, vol. 9)

Sechs Klavierstücke, Grüße an die Jugend
(1943, Breitkopf & Härtel)

Drei Albumblätter (Allegretto grazioso, Miniatur Gavotte, Andante)
(1933, *Zeitschrift für Musik,* Jahrgang 100, Notenbeilage. 3; Breitkopf & Härtel Gesamtausgabe, vol. 12)

An der schönen blauen Donau, Improvisation
(1930, Peters)

Liebestraum—Lyrisches Tonstück für Klavier
(1934, P.J. Tonger; Breitkopf & Härtel Gesamtausgabe, vol. 38)

Fünf Spezialstudien nach Chopin
(1899, Joseph Aibl Verlag; Universal Edition)

Vier Spezialstudien für die linke Hand
(1902, Joseph Aibl Verlag; Universal Edition)

Blätter und Blüten, 12 Klavierstücke
(1910, Paul Tschocher; Breitkopf & Härtel)

In der Nacht, Klavierstücke
(1902, in *Die Musik,* Erster Jahrgang, Heft 24, Fritz Schuberth; Breitkopf & Härtel Gesamtausgabe, vol. 12)

Perpetuum mobile (cis-moll)
(1905, C.F. Kahnt; Breitkopf & Härtel Gesamtausgabe, vol. 12)

Scherzo (fis-moll)
(1906, C.F. Kahnt; Breitkopf & Härtel Gesamtausgabe, vol. 12)

Caprice (fis-moll)
(1916, Kistner & Siegel; Breitkopf & Härtel Gesamtausgabe, vol. 12)

Kadenz zum 1. Satz von Mozart's Krönungskonzert D-dur, K.V. 537
(1986, Breitkopf & Härtel Gesamtausgabe, vol. 38)

Vier Klavierstücke (op. posth.)
(1901–06, E. Hoffmann, Otto Junne; Breitkopf & Härtel Gesamtausgabe, vol. 12)

Ewig Dein, Salonstück
> (1907, *Die Music*, 7. Jahrgang, Heft 1; Breitkopf & Härtel Gesamtausgabe, vol. 12)

Marsch der Stiftsdamen
> (1914, Luther; Breitkopf & Härtel Gesamtausgabe, vol. 12)

Fughette über das Deutschlandlied
> (1916, Deutsche Verlagsanstalt; Breitkopf und Härtel Gesamtausgabe, vol. 12)

CHRONOLOGICAL LIST OF WORKS FOR PIANO

OPUS	PIANO(S)	TITLE	COMPOSITION DATE
WoO	solo	*Präludium und Fuge g-moll*	(?)1890
WoO	solo	*Grande Valse de Concert*	1891
9	duet	*Zwölf Walzer-Capricen*	1892
10	duet	*Zwanzig Deutsche Tänze*	1893
11	solo	*Sieben Walzer*	1893
13	solo	*Lose Blätter, 14 kleine Klavierstücke*	1894
WoO	solo	*111 Kanons durch alle Dur- und Molltonarten*	1895
17	solo	*Aus der Jugendzeit, 20 kleine Klavierstücke*	1895
18	solo	*Improvisationen, 8 Klavierstücke*	(?)1896
WoO	solo	*Etude Brillante* (originally part of op. 18)	1896
20	solo	*Fünf Humoresken*	1898
22	duet	*Sechs Walzer*	1898
WoO	solo	*Sechs Klavierstücke, Grüße an die Jugend*	1898
WoO	solo	*Allegretto Grazioso*	1898
WoO	solo	*Miniatur Gavotte*	1898

(WoO: without opus number)

OPUS	PIANO(S)	TITLE	COMPOSITION DATE
WoO	solo	*An der schönen blauen Donau, Improvisation*	1898
WoO	solo	*Liebestraum—Lyrisches Tonstück für Klavier*	1898
24	solo	*Six Morceaux pour le Piano*	1898
25	solo	*Aquarelle, kleine Tonbilder*	1898
26	solo	*Sieben Fantasiestücke*	1898
32	solo	*Sieben Charakterstücke*	1899
WoO	solo	*Andante* (E. v. B.)	1899
34	duet	*Cinq Pièces Pittoresques*	1899
WoO	solo	*Fünf Spezialstudien nach Chopin*	1899
WoO	solo	*Vier Spezialstudien für die linke Hand*	1899
36	solo	*Bunte Blätter, 9 kleine Stücke*	1899
44	solo	*Zehn kleine Vortragsstücke zum Gebrauch beim Unterricht*	1900
45	solo	*Sechs Intermezzi*	1900
53	solo	*Silhouetten, 7 Stücke*	1900
58	duet	*Sechs Burlesken*	1901
WoO	solo	*Blätter und Blüten, 12 Klavierstücke*	1900–02
WoO	solo	*In der Nacht, Klavierstück*	1902
79a	solo	*Zehn Klavierstücke*	1901–03
81	solo	*Variationen und Fuge über ein Thema von J.S. Bach*	1904
82/I	solo	*Aus meinem Tagebuch*, vol. I	1904
86	two pianos	*Variationen und Fuge über ein Thema von Ludwig van Beethoven*	1904
89/1	solo	*Sonatine e-moll*	1905
89/2	solo	*Sonatine D-dur*	1905
WoO	solo	*Perpetuum mobile cis-moll*	1905
82/II	solo	*Aus meinem Tagebuch*, vol. II	1906
WoO	solo	*Scherzo fis-moll*	1906
WoO	solo	*Caprice fis-moll*	1906
WoO	solo	*Kadenz zum Krönungskonzert K.V.537*	1906
WoO	solo	*Vier Klavierstücke (op. posth.)*	1901–06
94	duet	*Sechs Stücke*	1906
96	two pianos	*Introduktion, Passacaglia und Fuge*	1906

OPUS	PIANO(S)	TITLE	COMPOSITION DATE
99	solo	*Sechs Präludien und Fugen*	1906/07
WoO	solo	*Ewig Dein, Salonstück* (op. 17523)	1907
89/3	solo	*Sonatine F-dur*	1908
89/4	solo	*Sonatine a-moll*	1908
114	solo	*Klavierkonzert mit Orchester*	1910
115	solo	*Episoden, Klavierstücke für große und kleine Leute*	1910
82/III	solo	*Aus meinem Tagebuch*, vol. III	1911
82/IV	solo	*Aus meinem Tagebuch*, vol. IV	1912
WoO	solo	*Marsch der Stiftsdamen*	1914
132a	two pianos	*Variationen und Fuge über ein Thema von W.A. Mozart*	1914
134	solo	*Variationen und Fuge über ein Thema von G.Ph. Telemann*	1914
143	solo	*Träume am Kamin, 12 kleine Klavierstücke*	1915
WoO	solo	*Fughette über das Deutschlandlied*	1916

NOTES

PREFACE

1. William E. Grim, *Max Reger, A Bio-Bibliography* (Westport, Conn.: Green wood Press, 1988), pp. 7–8.

2. "...was das ins Feuerwerfen betrifft, so vernichte ich genug Sachen, die mir selbst nicht genügen und sende Ihnen *nur* das, was ich *ganz* zu vertreten imstande bin!" Reger to Lauterbach & Kuhn, October 5, 1903, in Susanne Popp, ed., *Max Reger: Briefe an die Verleger Lauterbach & Kuhn*, Part 1 (Bonn: Max-Reger-Institut, 1993), 12:214 ff.

3. "Ich erkläre hiermit meine opera 1 bis 19 und op. 25 für heillosen Blödsinn! Also ich bin ganz und gar dagegen!" Reger to Karl Straube, March 29, 1905, in Susanne Popp, ed., *Max Reger: Briefe an Karl Straube* (Bonn: Ferd. Dümm- lers Verlag, 1986), p. 85.

1 THE EPIGONAL REVOLUTIONARY

1. "Ich, der glühendste Verehrer Joh. Seb. Bachs, Beethovens und Brahms', sollte den Umsturz predigen! Was ich will, ist ja doch nur eine Weiterbildung dieses Stiles." Reger to Adalbert Lindner, April 11, 1897, in Adalbert Lindner, *Max Reger: Ein Bild seines Jugendlebens und künstlerischen Werdens* (Regensburg: Bosse, 1938), p. 356.

2. "Ich möchte die These wagen, daß Regers Liebe zu Bach durch das Prisma Johannes Brahms' ging." Helmut Wirth, "Der Einfluß von J.S. Bach auf Max

Regers Schaffen," in *Max Reger, Ein Symposium* (Wiesbaden: Breitkopf & Härtel, 1974), p. 8.

3. "Und daß ich mit der Programmusikhochflut nicht und niemals mitschwimmen werde, das steht in mir fest! Trotz meiner fast, unbegrenzten Hochschätzung Rich. Strauß gegenüber kann ich mich nie entschließen, in diesem Fahrwasser zu segeln." Reger to Joseph Loritz, July 26, 1901, in Lindner, *Max Reger*, p. 350.

4. Judith Nagley, "Max Reger," in *The New Oxford Companion to Music* (Oxford: Oxford University Press, 1983), 2:1551.

5. Ernst Brennecke, "The Two Reger Legends," *Musical Quarterly* (1922), p. 396.

6. ". . . Vorzüge: das stupende kompositionstechnische Können, der unerschöpfliche Reichtum des kontrapunktischen Kombinationsvermögens, die starke Erfindungskraft in Bezug auf neue und unerhörte harmonische Wendungen. . . ." Rudolf Louis, *Münchner Neueste Nachrichten*, April 10, 1904.

7. See Oswald Kühn in *Neue Musikzeitung* 31, no. 18 (1910), p. 379: "Und die kolossale Produktivität Regers ist nicht unnatürlich an sich, sie hatte nur deshalb etwas Ungewöhnliches und manchmal 'Unheimliches', weil alles, was Reger schrieb, sofort auch gedruckt und aufgeführt wurde."

8. "In der schöpferischen Kraft, der rhythmischen Vielfalt der Erfindung und dem alle harmonischen Konsequenzen ziehenden Reichtum der thematischen Umgestaltung dieser Variationen steht Reger auf einer Höhe, die nur von den größten Meistern dieser Gattung erreicht worden ist." Richard Specht, *Die Zeit,* Vienna, February 21, 1905.

9. Fritz Stein, *Max Reger* (Potsdam: Athenaion, 1939). See also Hermann Unger, *Max Reger, Darstellung seines Lebens, Wesens und Schaffens* (Munich: Drei Masken Verlag, 1921); Guido Bagier, *Max Reger* (Stuttgart/Berlin: Deutsche Verlagsanstalt, 1923); Karl Hasse, *Max Reger, Mensch und Werk* (Berlin: Bote & Bock, 1938); and Rainer Cadenbach, *Max Reger und seine Zeit* (Regensburg: Laaber-Verlag, 1991).

2 A TUMULTUOUS LIFE

1. "Außerdem hat man nicht in völliger Verkennung des 'Absolut Musikalischen' fast jahrzehntelang gerade gegen unsere reichsten lebensvollsten Kunstformen, wie z. B. Fuge, Passacaglia gewettert . . . Glauben Sie mir, es sind Anzeichen da, daß wir wieder gesunden, daß der 'Nebel' der Symphonischen Dichtung, der all die, die nichts gelernt haben, auf unentwirrbare Abwege gebracht hat, sich lichtet." Reger to Georg Stern, January 12, 1910, in Else von Hase-Koehler, ed., *Max Reger: Briefe eines Deutschen Meisters—Ein Lebensbild* (Leipzig: Köhler & Amelang, 1928), p. 221.

2. "Seit jeher durch Kritik verletzbar, dürften Reger viele seiner Probleme jedoch in Wahrheit zunächst aus der eigenen Mißgunst gegen jeglichen Erfolg eines

vermeintlichen Konkurrenten, dann aus der grenzenlosen Unsicherheit bezüglich der eigenen Werke . . . und schließlich aus der hieraus resultierenden und zumindest verbal hemmungslosen Aggressivität entstanden sein." Rainer Cadenbach, *Max Reger und seine Zeit* (Regensburg: Laaber-Verlag, 1991), pp. 111–12.

3. " . . . da ich jetzt mit teuflischer Bosheit daran gehen werde, die Herren in ihrem eigenen Lager (wie Bremen) anzugreifen. . . ."
"... die Kerle so *niederbügeln* daß sie nicht mehr *papp* sagen können. . . ."
"... *Rache für die Zeit, in der die Gesellschaft* mich straflos musikalisch pervers erklärt hat, *muß* genommen werden und zwar *gründliche* Rache; *musikalisch* töten, das *muß* geschehen." Reger to Lauterbach & Kuhn, Sept. 16, 1906, in Ottmar Schreiber, ed., *Max Reger: Briefe zwischen der Arbeit* (Bonn: Ferd. Dümmlers Verlag, 1973), p. 78.

4. Adalbert Lindner, *Max Reger: Ein Bild seines Jugendlebens und künstlerischen Werdens* (Regensburg: Bosse, 1938).

5. Hugo Riemann, ed., *Musik-Lexikon* (Leipzig: M. Hesse, 1905).

6. Max Reger, *Beiträge zur Modulationslehre* (Leipzig: C.F. Kahnt, 1903).

7. See Cadenbach, *Max Reger und seine Zeit*, p. 281.

8. Max Reger, "Ich bitte ums Wort," *Neue Zeitschrift für Musik* 71, no. 2 (1904): 20 ff; and "Mehr Licht," *Neue Zeitschrift für Musik* 71, no. 11 (1904): 202 ff.

9. The program for this concert, which took place in the Singakademie Berlin on February 14, 1894, included the *Violinsonate*, op. 1, the *Klaviertrio*, op. 2, the 'Cellosonate', op. 5, and six selected songs.

10. See Cadenbach, *Max Reger und seine Zeit*, p. 38.

11. In the German term *Sturm und Drang*, well known in literature as well as in music, the word *Drang* is to be translated as something like "urging." The word *Tranck*, used instead by Reger, means "drinking."

12. "daß . . . Reger infolge Louis' heftiger Gegnerschaft jahrelang überhaupt ignoriert wurde." Oskar Kaul, *Die Musik in Geschichte und Gegenwart* (Kassel: Bärenreiter, 1960), 8:1232.

13. "Jenen verehrten Herrn Mitgliedern der *Max Reger Gemeinde*, die mich am Abend des 9. Februar durch eine *Serenade* erfreuten, bei der sie, soviel ich hören konnte, Bruchstücke aus der Sinfonietta ihres Meisters in höchst charakteristischer Weise brachten, erlaube ich mir auf diesem Wege meinen verbindlichsten Dank auszusprechen. München, den 10. Februar 1906, Rudolf Louis." *Münchner Neueste Nachrichten*, February 12, 1906.

14. " . . . Max Reger war der geborene Motoriker . . . mit eminenter Gabe im Erfassen der Notenkomplexe und der blitzschnellen Übertragung auf die Hand. . . ." Lindner, *Max Reger*, p. 32.

15. " . . . jedes große crescendo wurde (von Max Reger) dabei mit vorwärts drängendem Tempo im Sturm genommen, jedes Abebben im diminuendo

beruhigte auch das Zeitmaß wieder. . . ." Hermann Poppen, *Max Reger* (Leipzig: Breit-kopf & Härtel, 1918), p. 55.

16. ". . . daß Reger über genaueste Kenntnis der technischen Eigentümlichkeiten des Klavieres verfügte." Gerhard Wünsch, "Die Entwicklung des Klaviersatzes bei Max Reger" (Ph.D. diss., Universität Wien, 1950), p. 15.

17. Hugo Jinkertz, *Mit Reger an zwei Flügeln* (Düsseldorf: Die Fähre, 1951).

18. ". . . der sich in den Bach'schen Klavierkonzerten auch nicht immer streng an den Urtext hielt, vielmehr Füllstimmen und Oktav-Verdopplungen einfügend, seiner spontanen, genialen Eingebung folgte. . . ." Jinkertz, *Mit Reger an zwei Flügeln*, p. 15.

19. ". . . in seinen letzten Lebensjahren . . . für die Bewältigung der ungewöhnlichen Schwierigkeiten seiner großen Solo-Klavierwerke, wie der Bachvariationen oder des Klavierkonzertes war er, das klavierspielende Genie technisch keineswegs mehr gerüstet." *Ibid.*

20. Max Reger, "Offener Brief," *Die Musik* 7 (1907/08): 10–14; Max Reger, "Degeneration und Regeneration in der Musik," *Neue Musikzeitung* 29 (Stuttgart, 1907): 49–51.

21. ". . . eine spätere Zeit, wenn wir einmal *wieder gelernt* haben werden, daß Kunst und *Religion* im innersten Wesen *eins* sind, daß Kunst und Religion als *oberstes* und *einzig* zu erstrebendes Ziel *das* haben *sollen* und müssen: die Menschen zu veredeln, zu erheben, die Menschheit aus dem "Irdischen" zu befreien,—in dieser *nicht* mehr fernen Zeit wird man jene Abwege, jene grauenvollen Verirrungen, in denen die Künste unserer Zeit wandeln, mit Abscheu und tiefem Bedauern über den *Niedergang* des menschlichen Empfindens betrachten." Reger to Lauterbach & Kuhn, June 5, 1904 (in reference to the *Sinfonia Domestica* by R. Strauss), in Susanne Popp, ed., *Max Reger: Briefe an die Verleger Lauterbach & Kuhn*, Part 1 (Bonn: Ferd. Dümmlers Verlag, 1993), p. 324.

22. (1) (2) *Münchner Neueste Nachrichten*, February 7, 1903; (3) *Münchener Neueste Nachrichten*, April 10, 1904; (4) *Tagespost Graz*, Morgenblatt, January 16, 1907; (5) *Berliner Lokal-Anzeiger*, no. 511, October 7, 1908; (6) *Heidelberger Tageblatt*, no. 38, February 14, 1905; (7) *Allgemeine Musikzeitung* 36 (1909), no. 46.

23. Reger's students in Munich and Leipzig included such illustrous names as Othmar Schoeck, Joseph Haas, Karl Hasse, Hermann Grabner, Alexander Berrsche, Hermann Keller, Fritz Lubrich, Hermann Unger, and many others.

24. "Entgegen dem geläufigen Bild aber, gemäß dem dieser ganze Bereich [Ehrungen und Titel] ihm im Grunde herzlich gleichgültig gewesen sei, war sein Ehrgeiz auf. . . . selbst die äußerlichsten aller äußeren Anzeichen öffentlicher Wertschätzung durchaus beträchtlich." Cadenbach, *Max Reger und seine Zeit*, p. 121.

25. "... und jetzt *beginnt* der *freie Jenaische* Stil bei Reger." Reger to Karl Straube, April 7, 1915, in Susanne Popp, ed., *Max Reger: Briefe an Karl Straube* (Bonn: Ferd. Dümmlers Verlag, 1973), p. 249.

3 A STYLISTIC ENIGMA

1. "Max Reger unquestionably wrote too much music and almost every work of his ... is stuffed far too full of notes and especially accidentals. His work on the whole is oppressively deficient in light and air. But he was in a sense a great as well as a too abundantly creative musician. What has earned him lasting respect ... was not his pretended newness or any fundamental originality, but his tenacious upholding of the great traditions of composition, based mainly on a study of Bach's art in all its bearings." "Max Reger," in *Grove's Dictionary of Music and Musicians*, 5th ed. (London: Macmillan, 1970), 7:94.

2. "... musikalische Prosa ist hier weites Fortströmen realisiert mit den Mitteln spätromantischer Chromatik." Hermann Danuser, *Musikalische Prosa: Studien zur Musikgeschichte des 19. Jahrhunderts* (Regensburg: Bosse, 1975), 46:119–24.

3. Rainer Cadenbach, *Max Reger und seine Zeit* (Regensburg: Laaber-Verlag, 1991), p. 289.

4. "Woher soll nun das wirkliche Verstehen für meine Harmonik kommen, die so willkürlich scheinbar und doch so absolut logisch ist?" Reger to Georg Stern, January 12, 1912, in Else von Hase-Koehler, ed., *Max Reger: Briefe eines Deutschen Meisters—Ein Lebensbild* (Leipzig, Köhler & Amelang, 1928), p. 221.

5. "... Formgestaltung [bei Max Reger] ist der Hang zum Zuständlichen und zum natürlichen Wachsen aus einem Zustand in den anderen. ..." Alexander Berrsche, *Trösterin Musika* (Munich, G.D. Callwey, 1942).

6. "... Neigung zu äußerlicher Komplikation der Faktur und zur Überladung des technischen Apparates ... häuft bewußt die letzten harmonischen Wagnisse und modulatorischen Willkürlichkeiten in einer Weise, welche dem Hörer das Miterleben zur Unmöglichkeit macht ... Überreichtum als lästige, stereotype Manier. ..." "Max Reger," in Hugo Riemann, ed., *Musik-Lexikon*, 6th ed. (Leipzig: M. Hesse, 1905).

7. Gerd Sievers, *Die Grundlagen Hugo Riemanns bei Max Reger* (Wiesbaden: Breitkopf & Härtel, 1967).

8. "Der hastige Akkordwechsel fordert einerseits zu koloristischem (nicht funktionellem) Hören heraus, das aber andrerseits durch den spröden Charakter der Musik und die glanzlose Instrumentation gehemmt wird, sodaß man sich zurückgeworfen fühlt auf den Versuch, die musikalische Logik gewissenhaft nachzuvollziehen, ein Versuch, der jedoch daran scheitert, daß sich die har

monischen Ereignisse überstürzen." Carl Dahlhaus, "Warum ist Regers Musik so schwer verständlich?" in *Neue Zeitschrift für Musik*, 134th year (1973), 3:134. Also in *Musik und Bildung* 5 (1973): 677.

9. "Pfitzner [hat] die Überlastung der Werke Regers mit Ausdrucksbezeichnungen kritisiert." Walter Kolneder, *Kongreßbericht "Musik im Unterricht"* 48, no. 10 (October 1957).

10. "Ja, die Fugenform hat mich ganz gefangen genommen." Adalbert Lindner, *Max Reger: Ein Bild seines Jugendlebens und künstlerischen Werdens* (Regensburg: Bosse, 1938), p. 65.

11. ". . . Max Reger galt als eine Art von *musikalischem Ingenieur*." Berrsche, *Trösterin Musika*, p. 389.

12. "Allerdings ist der Begriff 'Melodie' bei mir anders zu nehmen, anders zu klassifizieren. . . . Nun, Melodik im *gewöhnlichen* Sinne schreibe ich nicht . . . der Begriff der 'Melodik' basiert bei 99% aller Musiker darauf, daß die Melodie *kadenzmäßige* harmonische Grundlage hat." Reger to Lauterbach & Kuhn, March 14, 1903, in Susanne Popp, ed., *Max Reger: Briefe an die Verleger Lauterbach & Kuhn*, Part 1 (Bonn: Ferd. Dümmlers Verlag, 1993), 12:108.

13. "Man schäle nur einmal die Themen seiner Kammermusikwerke aus den schillernden harmonischen, rhythmischen und modulatorischen Umhüllungen heraus. In sehr vielen Fällen . . . bleiben unverständliche und anscheinend sinnlose Töneketten übrig, wenn man hier die Geigenstimmen alleine durchnimmt." Walter Niemann, "Max Reger als Klavierkomponist," *Neue Zeitschrift für Musik*, 72nd year (October 25, 1905): 871.

14. *111 Kanons durch alle Dur- und Molltonarten* (1895).

15. As mentioned in Lindner, *Max Reger*, p. 137.

16. ". . . Reaktion Regers auf eine wachsende 'Trivialisierung' des musikalischen Materials ist die Technik der Polyphonisierung. Die Hauptstimme eines Satzes soll im Verbund mit anderen bewegten Stimmen gehört werden, welche alle melodisch, nämlich überwiegend stufenweise geführt sind." Martin Möller, *Untersuchungen zur Satztechnik Max Regers* (Wiesbaden: Breitkopf & Härtel, 1984), p. 57.

17. A signed handwritten note contains the BACH motif followed by "ist Anfang und Ende aller Musik—7. Mai 1902." Collection of the Max-Reger-Institut in Bonn.

18. ". . . mein Klaviersatz ist ganz ähnlich wie der Brahms'sche; die Figuration, die ich so liebe, zwei zu drei usw., die Verdoppelung der Terz, die Behandlung der linken Hand, die immer auf der Reise ist zwischen Bass, Tenor und Alt— das Ganze ist weiter nichts als durchbrochener, zum Teil orchestraler Klaviersatz. . . ." Lindner, *Max Reger*, p. 360.

19. ". . . [eine] 'Interpretation', bei der ein Werk ante factum zu Inspirationsquelle und Modell für ein neues Werk wird." Zofia Lissa, ed., "Max Regers Meta

morphosen der 'Berceuse' op. 57 von Frédéric Chopin," in *Max-Reger-Festschrift 1973* [*Südthüringer Forschungen*, October 1974] (Meiningen: Staatliche Museen Meiningen, 1974), p. 26.

4 A VACILLATING OEUVRE

1. Rainer Cadenbach, *Max Reger und seine Zeit* (Regensburg: Laaber-Verlag, 1991), p. 152.

2. "Keine einzige Note von all meinen bei Augener erschienenen schrecklichen Jugendsünden darf nach Deutschland angekauft werden! Ich bitte Dich aufs dringenste, daß Du bei Peters all' Deinen Einfluß aufbietest, daß nichts von Augener gekauft wird!" Reger to Karl Straube, March 29, 1905, in Susanne Popp, ed., *Max Reger: Briefe an Karl Straube* (Bonn: Ferd. Dümmlers Verlag, 1973).

3. "Die Resignation (op. 26, 5), das Menuett (op. 24, 2), das Scherzo (op. 44, 6) —bitte ich Sie *dringend nicht* mehr zu spielen, diese Musik ist für mich vollkommen *veraltet.* . . ." Reger to Henriette Schelle, November 21, 1901, in *Veröffentlichungen des Max-Reger-Instituts* (Bonn: 1950), 2:47.

4. William T. Hopkins, "The Short Piano Compositions of Max Reger (1873–1916)," Ph.D. diss., Indiana University, 1972.

5. See note 3 in the Preface and note 2 in this chapter.

6. ". . . Walzer, die ohne jegliche künstlerische Anteilnahme lediglich als Geschenk (wie auch die *Losen Blätter*) von mir an Augener für die beigesteuerten 200 Mark zum Konzerte zu betrachten sind." Reger to Adalbert Lindner, March 8, 1894, in Else von Hase-Koehler, ed., *Max Reger: Briefe eines Deutschen Meisters—Ein Lebensbild* (Leipzig: Köhler & Amelang, 1928), p. 37.

7. Willy Rehberg, ed., *Max Reger, Jugend Album für Klavier* (Wiesbaden: Schott, 1931). This collection contains 14 pieces in two volumes.

8. "Brahms ist die große Walhalla, die wir heute haben." Reger to Adalbert Lindner, July 20, 1891, in Else von Hase-Koehler, ed., *Max Reger*, p. 26.

9. This is nicely characterized by an anecdote according to which someone who was asked his opinion of a Max Reger concert answered, "Well, the usual— two slurred and two detached."

10. According to Lindner, Max Reger was imagining in the pseudo-polyphonic middle section a kind of procession of local dignitaries, wherein the tenor horn suddenly plays the wrong note F instead of F sharp (mm. 25–26), followed by the melody of a jocular song ("Du bist verrückt mein Kind"), beginning in m. 27. Adalbert Lindner, *Max Reger: Ein Bild seines Jugendlebens und künstlerischen Werdens* (Regensburg: Bosse, 1938). Reger himself called this composition "ein mißglücktes Ding" ("an unfortunate thing") and urged Lindner not to include it in any program.

11. *Aus meinem Tagebuch*, op. 82, nos. 3 and 5 (Teldec WE 28 004 B); op. 20,

no. 5; op. 45, no. 3; and op. 53, no. 2 (Telefunken HT 38, from "Berühmte Komponisten spielen eigene Werke," recorded in 1905). See also a recording attached to the catalogue of the exhibition in Bonn, "Reger in seiner Zeit," ed. by Siegfried Kross (Bonn: 1973).

12. ". . . bitte ich Sie *dringenst nicht* mehr zu spielen, diese Musik ist für mich völlig veraltet. . . ." Reger to Henriette Schelle, November 21, 1901, in *Veröffentlichungen des Max-Reger-Instituts* (Bonn: 1950), 2:47.

13. "Eine wahrhaft geglückte Synthese Liszt'scher Klavierformen und Brahms'-schem Geist in dennoch persönlicher Haltung." Gerhard Wünsch, "Die Entwicklung des Klaviersatzes bei Max Reger" (Ph.D. diss., Universität Wien, 1950), p. 59.

14. ". . . um nicht den Eindruck zu erwecken, daß ich 'voll und ganz' rechne, habe ich extra den Zusatz 'Zum Gebrauche beim Unterricht' gemacht. Schlecht is es ja nicht, aber ich betrachte solche Opera aus meiner Feder mit gemischten Gefühlen. . . ." Reger to Alexander Wilhelm Gottschalg, April 16, 1900, in Else von Hase-Koehler, ed., *Max Reger*, p. 70.

15. ". . . [stellt dar] eine Auflockerung des romantisch-harmonischen Klavierstils zu linear bestimmter, diffiziler Nuancierung des Anschlags erfordernder, dynamisch reich schattierter Satzweise persönlichster Prägung." Wünsch, "Die Entwicklung des Klaviersatzes bei Max Reger," p. 77.

16. ". . . daß ihm als Werk gerade nicht der Text galt . . . [er] bildet nur eine Spur, die den Weg zum ihm [dem Werk] andeutet." Cadenbach, *Max Reger und seine Zeit,* p. 202.

17. "Einzelne charakteristische Motive mit besonderem Ausdrucks- oder Spannungsgehalt treten in den einzelnen Variationen in den Vordergrund der Betrachtung, werden neu belichtet, ihre letzten Möglichkeiten ausgenutzt zur Gestaltung von musikalischen Gebilden, die, aus dem Zusammenhang gerissen, keine Beziehung zum Thema mehr aufweisen." Wünsch, "Die Entwicklung des Klaviersatzes bei Max Reger," pp. 93–94.

18. ". . . . eine Musik vorschwebte, die nicht mehr den traditionellen Kategorien der Variation gehorchte." Elmar Budde, "Zeit und Form in Max Regers Variationen und Fuge über ein Thema von Johann Sebastian Bach," in *Reger Studien 3*, edited by Susanne Popp and Susanne Shigihara (Wiesbaden: Max-Reger-Institut, 1988), p. 129.

19. "Ich bitte alle Metronomangaben nicht als strikte bindend anzusehen; doch dürften die Metronomangaben besonders bei den bewegten (schnellen) Variationen und hauptsächlich bei der Fuge, der ein breites Tempo immer gelegen sein wird, als die überhaupt höchst zulässigen Tempi in Bezug auf 'Schnelligkeit' gelten, wenn nicht der Vortrag auf Kosten der Deutlichkeit leiden soll." Footnote on the first page of the autograph copy.

20. Incidentally, given Reger's imaginative powers, it seems only natural that

splinters of the theme by Bach appear *nolens volens*, here and there (for example, in mm. 321–322 and 325–326).

21. "Eine Analyse des Schaffensprozesses . . . wird an den privatschriftlichen Entwürfen eine zunehmende Tendenz zur völlig unverhüllten 'Montage' finden: Takte und ganze Werkteile werden herausgeschnitten und eliminiert oder an anderer Stelle wieder eingesetzt." Cadenbach, *Max Reger und seine Zeit*, p. 199.

22. ". . . auch da ersetzt in den 'rationell-materialistisch' bestimmten letzten Bänden gar oft Routine und überlegene Technik den impulsiven Einfall. . . ." Wünsch, "Die Entwicklung des Klaviersatzes bei Max Reger," p. 157.

23. "Mit der Reduktion des Motivischen auf wenige austauschbare Elemente prägt eine mechanische und im modernen Sinne technische Dimension den Kompositionsprozeß. Das musikalische Detail hat keine Kraft mehr und wird zum musikalischen Baustein." Roman Brotbeck, *Zum Spätwerk von Max Reger (Fünf Diskurse)*, Schriftenreihe des Max-Reger-Institutes Bonn (Wiesbaden: Breitkopf & Härtel, 1988), p. 49.

24. ". . . meine Musik ist nichts für jene, die schwach im Magen sind . . . ich ziehe Dissonanzragout vor. . . ." Reger to Emil Krause, May 8, 1902, in Else von Hase-Koehler, ed., *Max Reger*, p. 95.

25. In *Denkmäler Deutscher Tonkunst*, vol. 61–62 (Wiesbaden: Breitkopf & Härtel, 1958–).

26. ". . . [ist] man versucht, von einem Kompendium Regerscher Klaviertechnik überhaupt zu sprechen." Wünsch, "Die Entwicklung des Klaviersatzes bei Max Reger," p. 201.

27. "Ich glaube mit ruhigem Gewissen sagen zu können, daß seit Brahms' *Händelvariationen kein* derartiges Werk mehr geschaffen worden ist. . . . Op 134 ist zweifellos mein bisheriges *bestes* Klavierwerk." Reger to his publisher, N. Simrock, August 21, 1914, in Ottmar Schreiber, ed., *Max Reger: Briefe zwischen der Arbeit* (Bonn: Ferd. Dümmlers Verlag, 1973), p. 243.

28. "Von einer Bezeichnung des Fingersatzes habe ich absichtlich Abstand genommen, da der Spieler, der diese Specialstudien übt oder öffentlich vorträgt, über die Prinzipien des Fingersatzes längst hinaus ist, und ich auch in dieser Beziehung die künstlerische Freiheit eines jeden respektieren wollte. Es wird aber von Nutzen sein, die Studien *legato* and *staccato* getrennt zu üben." Max Reger, *Fünf Specialstudien* (Leipzig: Jos. Aibl Verlag, 1899), footnote p. 18.

5 THE INTERPRETIVE FACTOR

1. "Vor Antritt seines Hofkapellmeisteramts erklärt Reger dem Herzog von Meiningen schon einmal deutlich, er sei *gezwungen zu concertieren*, um für den Vortrag seiner Werke eine 'Tradition' zu begründen." Ottmar Schreiber, *Max Reger in seinen Konzerten*, (Bonn: Ferd. Dümmlers Verlag, 1981), 1:7.

2. "In der Temponahme läßt er sich ganz von der Empfindung des Augenblicks leiten. . . ." C.W., in *Aachener Anzeiger* 236 (October 10, 1911).

3. ". . . wie er immer auf ganz eigenartige, dabei höchst natürliche Weise phrasierte, das Wichtigste hervorhob, die *lebhaften Mittelstimmen zurück-drängte. . . .*" Joseph Marx, *Betrachtungen eines romantischen Realisten* (Wien: 1947), p. 306, cited in Wünsch, "Die Entwicklung des Klaviersatzes bei Max Reger" (Ph.D. diss., Universität Wien, 1950), p. 12.

4. "(man) . . . sehnte sich nach dem Glanz des Regerschen Anschlages, seinem hingehauchten pianissimo, dieser letzten Nüance zwischen Ton und Stille, seinem agogisch belebten Vortrag der das spröde Klavier atmen und singen läßt. Gerade der Mangel verständnisvoll belebender agogischer Unterstrei-chung berühren besonders peinlich. . . ." Alexander Berrsche, *Augsburger Postzeitung*, October 14, 1907.

5. "Allen die Regers Klaviermusik näher kommen wollen, wäre das Studium dieser eigenartigen, fast durchweg das Legato bevorzugenden Vortragsart, die manchen schrulligen Ausdruck durchaus natürlich erscheinen läßt, zu empfehlen. . . ." Paul Bekker, *Allgemeine Zeitung Berlin* 37, no. 10 (1910), p. 244.

6. "Also Du weißt: ich spiele *nur Ibach*; die Fabrik baut ganz hervorragend schöne Flügel und stellt überall die besten Instrumente *kostenlos* zur Verfü-gung." Reger to Philipp Wolfrum, September 22, 1910, in Ottmar Schreiber, ed., *Max Reger: Briefe zwischen der Arbeit* (Bonn: Ferd. Dümmlers Verlag, 1973), p. 159.

7. Excerpt from Hermann Hesse, *Musik* (Frankfurt/Main: Suhrkamp, 1986), pp. 42–43: "Ludwig spielte, und sie sah eine weite dunkle Wasserfläche in großen Takten wogen. Eine Schar von großen, gewaltigen Vögeln kam mit brausenden Flügelschlägen daher, urweltlich düster. Der Sturm tönte dumpf und warf zuweilen schaumige Wellenkämme in die Luft, die in viele kleine Perlen zerstäubten. In dem Brausen der Wellen, des Windes und der großen Vogelflügel klang etwas Geheimes mit, da sang bald mit lautem Pathos bald mit feiner Kinderstimme ein Lied, eine innige, liebe Melodie.

"Wolken flatterten schwarz und in zerrissenen Strähnen, dazwischen gin-gen wundersame Blicke in golden tiefe Himmel auf. Auf großen Wogen ritten Meerscheusale von grausamer Bildung, aber auf kleinen Wellen spielten zarte, rührende Reigen von Engelbüblein mit komisch dicken Gliedern und mit Kinderaugen. Und das Gräßliche ward vom Lieblichen mit wachsendem Zauber überwunden, und das Bild verwandelte sich in ein leichtes, luftiges, der Schwere enthobenes Zwischenreich, wo in einem eigenen, mondähnlichen Lichte ganz zarte, schwebende Elfenwesen Luftreigen tanzten und dazu mit reinen, kristallenen, körperlosen Stimmen selig leichte, leidlos verwehende Töne sangen.

"Nun aber wurde es, als seien es nicht mehr die engelhaften Lichtelfen sel ber, die im weißen Scheine sangen und schwebten, sondern als sei es der Mensch, der von ihnen erzählte oder träumte.

"Ein schwerer Tropfen Sehnsucht und unstillbares Menschenleid rann in die verklärte Welt des wunschlos Schönen, statt des Paradieses entstand des Menschen Traum vom Paradies, nicht weniger glänzend und schön, aber von tiefen Lauten unstillbaren Heimwehs begleitet."

(English translation by Helen Milne and Garrett Epp.)

SELECTED DISCOGRAPHY

Based on information provided in William E. Grim, *Max Reger: A Bio-Bibliography* (Westport, Conn.: Greenwood Press, 1988).

ArtDir 20: *Bach Variations*, op. 81 (Gunnar Johansen, piano).

CBS S 72402: *Piano Concerto*, op. 114 (Rudolf Serkin, piano; Philadelphia Orchestra, Eugene Ormandy, conductor).

Da Camera MRK 19734: *Works for Piano I*: opp. 9, 10, 22, 34, 58, 81, 82, 86, 89, 94, 96, 132a, 134 (Aloys and Alfons Kontarsky, Karl-Heinz and Michael Schlüter, Hugo Steurer, Richard Laugs, piano).

Da Camera MRK 19735: *Works for Piano II*: opp. 11, 13, 17, 18, 20, 24, 25, 26, 32, 36, 44, 45, 53, 79a, 99, 115, 143, works without opus number (Richard Laugs, Wilfried Kassebaum, piano).

Da Camera Magna 93123: *4 Sonatinas*, op. 89 (Wilfried Kassebaum, piano).

Da Camera Magna SM 93131: *"An der schönen blauen Donau"; Etude brillante in C Minor; Scherzo and Caprice in F-sharp Minor; Four Special Studies for the left hand alone; Improvisation in C Minor; Perpetuum mobile in C Major; Perpetuum mobile in C-sharp Minor* (Hans-Dieter Bauer, piano).

Danachord DACO-225: *Aus meinem Tagebuch*, op. 82, no. 1 (Niels Vigge Bentzon).

Electrola 1 C 053–28925 and Electrola E 80439: *Piano Concerto*, op. 114 (Erik Thenbergh, piano; Südwestfunk Orchestra, Hans Rosbaud, conductor).

Eurodisc 86 474 KK: Bach Variations, op. 81; *Träume am Kamin*, op. 143, nos. 1, 3, 4, 7, and 10 (Dieter Zechlin, piano).

Eurodisc 86 475 KK: Piano Concerto, op. 114 (Amadeus Webersinke, piano; Dresden Philharmonic Orchestra, Günther Herbig, conductor).

Garnet G 40 125: Introduction, Passacaglia and Fugue, op. 96 (Max Martin Stein and Hansjörg von Löw, piano).

Leonarda 113: Piano Concerto, op. 114 (Steven Mayer, piano; Hague Philharmonic Orchestra, Ernest Bour, conductor).

Musical Heritage Society MHS 1268: Telemann Variations, op. 134; *Mozart Variations*, op. 132a (Alfons and Aloys Kontarsky, Hugo Steurer, piano).

Musical Heritage Society MHS 1292: Beethoven Variations, op. 86; *Introduction, Passacaglia, and Fugue*, op. 96 (Alfons and Aloys Kontarsky).

Musical Heritage Society MHS 1487: Pièces pittoresques, op. 34; *Six Burlesques*, op. 58; *Six Pieces*, op. 94 (Karl-Heinz and Michael Schlüter, piano).

Musical Heritage Society MHS 1618: Twenty German Dances, op. 10; *Six Waltzes*, op. 22 (Karl-Heinz and Michael Schlüter, piano).

Musical Heritage Society MHS 1619: Waltz-Caprices, op. 9 (Karl-Heinz and Michael Schlüter, piano).

Musical Heritage Society MHS 1620/22: Aus meinem Tagebuch, op. 82 (Richard Laugs, piano).

Musical Heritage Society MHS 1867: Bach Variations, op. 81; *Humoresques*, op. 20; *Silhouettes*, op. 53 (Richard Laugs, piano).

Musical Heritage Society MHS 4136: Episodes, op. 115 [among various other works] (Richard Laugs, piano).

Orion ORS 73130: Pièces pittoresques, op. 34; *Six Waltzes*, op. 22; *Six pieces*, op. 94 (Sharon Gunderson and Jo Ann Smith, piano).

Orion 77281: Beethoven Variations, op. 86 (Evelinde Trenkner and Vladimir Pleshakov, pianos).

Orion OC-679: Telemann Variations, op. 134 (Evelinde Trenkner, piano).

Teldec WE 28 004 B: Aus meinem Tagebuch, op. 82, no. 3, *Andante sostenuto* in D Major, and no. 5, *Moderato*, also called *Gavotte in E Major* (Max Reger, piano).

Telefunken HT 38: Humoreske, op. 20, no. 5; *Intermezzo*, op. 45, no. 3; *Silhouette*, op. 53, no. 2 (Max Reger, piano) [From *Berühmte Komponisten spielen eigene Werke*, recorded in 1905].

SELECTED BIBLIOGRAPHY

BIOGRAPHIES

Bagier, Guido. *Max Reger*. Stuttgart/Berlin: Deutsche Verlagsanstalt, 1923.

Hase-Koehler, Else von, ed. *Max Reger: Briefe eines Deutschen Meisters—Ein Lebensbild*. Leipzig: Köhler & Amelang, 1928.

Hasse, Karl. *Max Reger*. Leipzig: Siegel, 1921.

———. *Max Reger*. Dortmund: Verlag W. Crüwell, 1951.

Kallenberg, Siegfried. *Max Reger*. Leipzig: Reclam, 1929.

Lindner, Adalbert. *Max Reger: Ein Bild seines Jugendlebens und künstlerischen Werdens*. Regensburg: Bosse, 1938.

Poppen, Hermann. *Max Reger*. Leipzig: Breitkopf & Härtel, 1918.

Reger, Elsa. *Mein Leben mit und für Max Reger*. Leipzig: Köhler & Amelang, 1930.

Stein, Fritz. *Max Reger*. Potsdam: Athenaion, 1939.

Unger, Hermann. *Max Reger*. Leipzig: Velhagen & Klasing, 1924.

———. *Max Reger: Darstellung seines Lebens, Wesens und Schaffens*. Munich: Drei Masken, 1921.

Wirth, Helmut. *Max Reger in Selbstzeugnissen und Bilddokumenten*. Hamburg: Rohwolt, 1973.

BOOKS CONTAINING IMPORTANT REFERENCES TO MAX REGER

Berrsche, Alexander. *Trösterin Musika*. Munich: Callwey, 1942.

Brotbeck, Roman. *Zum Spätwerk Max Regers (Fünf Diskurse)*. Wiesbaden: [Max-Reger-Institut] Breitkopf & Härtel, 1988.

Danuser, Hermann. *Musikalische Prosa. Studien zur Musikgeschichte des 19. Jahrhunderts*, vol. 46. Regensburg: Bosse, 1975.

Jinkertz, Willi. *Mit Reger an zwei Flügeln*. Düsseldorf: Verlag Die Fähre, 1951.

Klaus, Kenneth B. *The Romantic Period in Music*. Boston: Allyn & Bacon, 1970.

Müller-Blattau, Josef. *Geschichte der Fuge*. 3rd ed. Kassel: Bärenreiter, 1963.

Nelson, Robert U. *The Technique of Variation: A Study of the Instrumental Variation from Antonio Cabezon to Max Reger*. Berkeley: University of California Press, 1962.

Niemann, Walter. *Die Musik der Gegenwart*. Berlin: Schuster & Loeffler, 1921.

Schmid-Lindner, August. *Ausgewählte Schriften*. Tutzing, 1973.

Wolters, Klaus, and Franzpeter Goebels. *Die Klaviermusik zu zwei Händen. Handbuch der Klavierliteratur*, vol. 1. Zurich: Atlantis, 1967.

ARTICLES

Abbreviations

AMZ	*Allgemeine Musikzeitung*. Berlin, 1874 ff.
Da	*Daheim*. Leipzig.
M	*Die Musik*. Berlin, 1901 ff.
MMRGes	*Mitteilungen der Max-Reger-Gesellschaft*. Bonn: 1921 ff.
MMRI	*Mitteilungen des Max-Reger-Instituts*. Bonn: 1954 ff.
MO	*Musical Opinion*.
MWbl	*Musikalisches Wochenblatt*. Leipzig, 1870 ff.
NMZ	*Neue Musikzeitung*. Stuttgart, 1880 ff.
NZFM	*Neue Zeitschrift für Musik*. Leipzig, 1834–1932; Regensburg, 1933 ff.
SiMW	*Signale für die musikalische Welt*. Berlin, 1842 ff.
SMZ	*Schweizerische Musikzeitung*

Blessinger, Karl. "Zur Metrik Max Regers." *MMRGes* 6 (1927): 5–9.

Böttcher, Lukas. "Bach, Reger und das Barock: Aphoristische Betrachtungen." *NZFM* 107 (1940): 137–38.

Brennecke, Ernest. "The Two Reger-Legends." *Musical Quarterly*, 1922, pp. 384–96.

Crew, Sidney. "Reger's Pianoforte Music." *MO*, 1912, pp. 761–63.

Dahlhaus, Carl. "Warum ist Regers Musik so schwer verständlich?" *NZFM* 134 (1973): 134.

Dilsner, Laurance. "Reger Can Be for Anyone." *Clavier* 12, no. 4 (1973): 11–12, 20-28.

Georgii, Walter. "Die Klaviermusik der letzten Jahrzehnte." *NMZ* 44 (1923): 230–32.

Grabner, Hermann. "Die Klaviermusik Max Regers." *Das Klavierspiel* 2, no. 5 (1960): 135–39.

Hecker, Joachim von. "Wie spielte Reger?" *Musica Schallplatte*, 1959, pp. 52–54.

Hehemann, Max. "Regers Klaviermusik." *NMZ* 37 (1916): 289.

Kwast, James. "Max Reger als Kammermusik- und Klavierkomponist." *AMZ* 37 (1910): 441–43.

Liebscher, Arthur. "Die Variationsform als Ausdrucksmittel bei Max Reger." *M* 8 (1908/09): 323–40.

Lindner, Adalbert. "Max Regers Klavierspiel." *MMRGes* 11 (1933): 1–6.

Lissa, Zofia. "Max Regers Metamorphosen der 'Berceuse' op. 57 von Frédéric Chopin." *Fontes Artis Musicae*, 1966, pp. 79–84.

Lowe, George. "The Piano Works of Reger." *MO*, 1915, p. 909.

Lüpke, G. von. "Hausmusik von Max Reger." *MWbl* 27 (1906): 345–47.

Mitscherlich-Claus, Luise, and Harald Kümmerling. "Schubert, Brahms und Reger: Eine Sinndeutung von Regers Silhouetten." *NZFM* 114 (1953): 148–51.

Niemann, Walter. "Max Reger als Klavierkomponist." *NZFM* 72, no. 44 (1905).

Pisk, Paul A. "Die Klavierwerke Max Regers." *SMZ* 68, no. 25 (1928).

———. "Max Regers Klavierstil." *MMRGes* 7 (1928): 5–8.

Reger, Max. "Ich bitte ums Wort." *NZFM* 71, no. 2 (1904).

———. "Mehr Licht." *NZFM* 71, no. 11 (1904).

Rehberg, Willi. "Reger als Klavierkomponist." *MMRGes* 8 (1932): 15–17.

Schenker, Heinrich. "Ein Gegenbeispiel: Max Reger, op. 81, Variationen und Fuge über ein Thema von Joh. Seb. Bach für Klavier." *Das Meisterwerk in der Musik: Ein Jahrbuch*, vol. 2. Munich, 1926, pp. 171–92.

Schreiber, Ottmar. "Regers Klavierspiel auf Schallplatten." *MMRI* 5 (1957): 37–38.

———. "Verzeichnis der im Musikalienhandel erhältlichen Werke Regers." *MMRI* 3 (1955): 25–28.

Segnitz, Eugen. "Hausmusik. Max Regers Klavierwerke." Part 1, *Da* 40, no. 20 (1903/04): 25. Part 2, *Da* 40, no. 23 (1903/04): 25.

Sievers, Gerd. "Zur Harmonik Regers." *MMRI* 7 (1958): 15–20.

[Sievers, Gerd]. "Regers zweihändige Klavierkompositionen: Form- und Stilkritische Untersuchung." Part 1, *MMRI* 11 (1960): 18–27. Part 2, *MMRI* 12 (1961): 14–23.

———. "Die Klavierkompositionen Max Regers." *MMRI* Sonderheft (1973): 34–43.

Swoboda, Heinrich. "Zu Regers Variationsstil/Analyse der Bach-Variationen Opus 81." *MMRGes* 4 (1924): 21–24.

Thiessen, Karl. "Max Reger: Op. 82/3, Aus meinem Tagebuch. Sechs kleine Stücke für Klavier zu 2 Händen." *SiMW* 70, no. 39 (1912):1272–73.

———. "Sechs Burlesken für Clavier zu vier Händen von Max Reger op. 58." *SiMW* 60, no. 41 (1902): 787–88.

———. "Silhouetten. Sieben Stücke für Clavier zu zwei Händen componiert von Max Reger." *SiMW* 60, no. 45/46 (1902): 887.

Unger, Hermann. "Regers Hausmusik." *MMRGes* 4 (1924): 12–14.

Wirth, Helmut. "Notizen zu Regers Klavierwerk." *MMRI* 3 (1955): 19–23.

———. "Max Reger und Edvard Grieg." *MMRI* 18 (1971): 38–47.

———. "Johannes Brahms und Max Reger." *Brahms-Studien* 1 (1974): 91–112.

Wolf, Gary. "The Piano Works of Max Reger." *The Music Director*, 1966, p. 11.

Wünsch, Gerhard. "Spielformen in Regers Klaviermusik." *MMRI* 18 (1971): 16–29.

DISSERTATIONS

Holliman, Jamesetta V. "A Stylistic Study of Max Reger's Solo Piano Variations and Fugues on Themes by Johann Sebastian Bach and Georg Philipp Telemann." Ph.D. diss., New York University, 1975.

Hopkins, William Thomas. "The Short Piano Compositions of Max Reger (1873–1916)." Ph.D. diss., Indiana University, 1972.

Schmitt, Hans. "Studien zur Geschichte und Stilistik des Satzes für zwei Klaviere zu vier Händen." Ph.D. diss., Saarbrücken, 1965.

Sievers, Gerd. "Die Grundlagen Hugo Riemanns bei Max Reger." Ph.D. diss., Hamburg, 1949.

Wolf, James Gary. "The Solo Pianoforte Variations of Max Reger." Ph.D. diss., University of Rochester, 1964.

Wolf, Margarete. "Das Capriccio in Regers Klaviermusik." Ph.D. diss., Universität Wien, 1928.

Wünsch, Gerhard. "Die Entwicklung des Klaviersatzes bei Max Reger." Ph.D. diss., Universität Wien, 1950.

INDICES